Carla Bardi

ice creams
& sorbets

ice creams • sorbets • granitas • cool desserts

APPLE

First published in the UK in 2012 by
Apple Press
7 Greenland Street
London NW1 0ND
United Kingdom
www.apple-press.com

This book was conceived, edited and designed by
McRae Publishing Ltd, London

NOTE TO OUR READERS
Eating eggs or egg whites that are not completely cooked poses the possibility
of salmonella food poisoning. The risk is greater for pregnant women, the elderly,
the very young, and persons with impaired immune systems. If you are concerned
about salmonella, you can use reconstituted powdered egg whites or pasteurized eggs.

Project Director Anne McRae
Art Director Marco Nardi

ICE CREAMS & SORBETS
Photography Brent Parker Jones
Text Carla Bardi
Editing Foreign Concept
Food Styling Lee Blaylock
Food Styling Assistant Rochelle Seator
Prop Styling Lee Blaylock
Layouts Filippo Delle Monache

ISBN 978-1-84543-443-4

Printed in China

contents

getting started

There are more than 100 delicious recipes in this book. Most of them are simple and require only basic skills and a few minutes to prepare. A few are quite challenging and will stretch your culinary know-how to the full. All recipes have been rated for difficulty: 1 (simple), 2 (fairly simple), or 3 (challenging). In these pages we have chosen 25 of the best recipes, just to get you started!

 SIMPLE

54

STRAWBERRY YOGURT sorbet

14

CREAM CHEESE
ice cream

36

DOUBLE CHOCOLATE
CHIP ice cream

48

ORANGE
sorbet

94

MILK CHOCOLATE
semifreddo

62

SAGE sorbet

69

STRAWBERRY
spumone

CHALLENGING

98

SICILIAN cassata

71

PEACH
granita

116

BIRTHDAY
ice cream cake

CLASSICS

RUM & RAISIN
ice cream

CHOCOLATE CHIP
ice cream

BLACK FOREST ice cream cake

LEMON SORBET
with strawberries

COFFEE
granita

CARDAMOM
ice cream

ROCKY ROAD
ice cream

EDITOR'S CHOICE

RICE CREAM with chocolate sauce

RASPBERRY
sorbet

MOJITO
granita

BEST ICE CREAM

AMARENA CHERRY
ice cream

BEST SORBET

BITTER CHOCOLATE
sorbet

BEST GRANITA

MELON
granita

BEST SEMIFREDDO

CHOCOLATE
MASCARPONE semifreddo

BEST ICE CREAM CAKE

ICE CREAM MERINGUE
torte

ice creams

PUMPKIN & AMARETTI COOKIE ice cream

4 pounds (2 kg) fresh pumpkin
$3/4$ cup (150 g) sugar
$1/8$ teaspoon salt
$12/3$ cups (400 ml) heavy (double) cream
2–3 drops bitter almond extract (essence)
About 20 amaretti cookies

Serves 4–6 • Preparation 15 minutes + 30 minutes to chill + time to churn • Cooking 5 minutes • Difficulty 1

1. Peel the pumpkin, remove the seeds, and slice. Steam until just tender, 8–10 minutes. Let cool and then lightly squeeze with your hands to remove as much moisture as possible.

2. Weigh out 1 pound (500 g) of pumpkin. Place in a food processor with the sugar and salt and chop until smooth.

3. Put the cream in a heavy-based saucepan over medium heat and bring to a boil. Remove from the heat and stir in the almond extract. Pour into a bowl with the pumpkin and stir well. Let cool completely, stirring often. Chill in the refrigerator for 30 minutes.

4. Transfer the mixture to an ice cream machine and freeze following the manufacturer's instructions.

5. Crumble half the amaretti cookies into serving bowls. Top with the ice cream and finish with an amaretti cookie.

If you liked this recipe, you will love these as well.

NOUGAT ICE CREAM with cognac

CARDAMOM ice cream

ICE CREAM with port & almond biscotti

People have been making ice cream since long before electricity was invented, so if you don't have an ice cream machine you can still make this delicious creamy dessert at home. Follow our instructions in the recipe below. All of the recipes in this book can be made without an ice cream machine in this same way.

VANILLA ice cream

4	cups (1 liter) milk
6	coffee beans
1	small (about 1-inch/2.5-cm long) cinnamon stick
	Small piece of organic lemon zest, removed using a sharp knife
1	large vanilla pod
$1/8$	teaspoon salt
5	large egg yolks
1	cup (200 g) sugar
$3/4$	teaspoon cornstarch (cornflour)
2	large egg whites

Serves 6 • Preparation 20 minutes + 30 minutes to chill + time to churn
Cooking 5–10 minutes • Difficulty 1

1. Combine $3^1/_2$ cups (875 ml) of milk in a heavy-based saucepan with the coffee beans, cinnamon, lemon zest, vanilla, and salt over medium heat. Mix well and bring to a boil. Decrease the heat to low and simmer gently for 5 minutes.

2. Beat the egg yolks, sugar, and cornstarch in a medium bowl with an electric mixer on high speed until pale and creamy.

3. With mixer on low, add the remaining $1/_2$ cup (125 ml) milk followed by the hot milk mixture. Return to the saucepan and simmer over very low heat, stirring constantly, for 2 minutes. Do not let the mixture boil. Remove from the heat and strain through a fine-mesh sieve into a bowl. Let cool, stirring often. Chill in the refrigerator for 30 minutes.

4. Beat 2 egg whites until stiff peaks form and fold them into the mixture just before you transfer it to your ice cream machine. Freeze following the manufacturer's instructions.

5. If you don't own an ice cream machine, pour the custard mixture into a freezer-proof container (made of plastic or stainless steel) and place in the freezer until it begins to freeze around the edges, about 45 minutes. Stir vigorously with a whisk or spoon or beat with a hand-held blender. Return to the freezer and leave for 30 minutes. Repeat this stirring and freezing sequence four or five more times, until the ice cream is smooth and creamy.

6. Transfer to a freezer-proof container and freeze until required.

MAKING ICE CREAM AT HOME

Preparing ice cream at home is simple, especially if you own an ice cream machine. The method is the same for all flavors; first you make a milk- or cream-based custard, then flavoring is added, before being tipped into an ice cream machine to churn. By making ice cream at home you can be sure that there are no preservatives or additives—just wholesome eggs, sugar, milk, and cream.

1. SIMMER 3¹/₂ cups (875 ml) of milk with the coffee, cinnamon, lemon zest, vanilla, and salt over medium-low heat.

2. BEAT the egg yolks, sugar, and cornstarch in a bowl with an electric mixer on high speed until pale and creamy.

3. ADD the remaining cold milk to the egg mixture then the hot milk mixture. Return to the pan and simmer over low heat, stirring constantly, for 2 minutes. Do not let the mixture boil.

4. REMOVE from the heat and strain through a fine-mesh sieve into a bowl. Let cool, stirring often. Refrigerate for 30 minutes.

5. BEAT 2 egg whites until stiff peaks form. Fold into the mixture. Transfer to an ice cream machine and churn.

This ice cream has a range of subtle flavors that are best enjoyed alone or with just a sprinkling of coarsely chopped nuts.

AROMATIC ice cream

2	cups (500 ml) milk
1$\frac{1}{3}$	cups (340 ml) heavy (double) cream
$\frac{1}{2}$	cup (100 g) sugar
$\frac{1}{3}$	cup (90 g) honey
	Zest of half an organic lemon, in one long piece, removed using a sharp knife
	Zest of half an organic orange, in one long piece, removed using a sharp knife
1	(2-inch/5-cm) cinnamon stick
30	coffee beans
$\frac{1}{8}$	teaspoon salt
1	ounce (30 g) skim milk powder
$\frac{1}{2}$	teaspoon vanilla extract (essence)
	Coarsely chopped walnuts, to garnish

Serves 4-6 • Preparation 30 minutes + 4-12 hours to infuse + 30 minutes to chill + time to churn • Cooking 5-10 minutes • Difficulty 1

1. Bring the milk and cream to a boil in a heavy-based saucepan over medium heat.

2. Remove from the heat and add the sugar, honey, lemon and orange zest, cinnamon, coffee beans, and salt. Let cool then chill in the refrigerator for 4 hours or overnight. Strain the mixture through a fine-mesh sieve.

3. Put the skim milk powder in a heavy-based saucepan and pour in the milk mixture. Stir over medium heat then, just before the mixture begins to boil, decrease the heat to low and simmer for 2 minutes.

4. Remove from the heat and stir in the vanilla. Beat with a whisk on medium speed until cool. Chill in the refrigerator for 30 minutes.

5. Beat with a whisk for 2–3 minutes. Transfer the mixture to your ice cream machine and freeze following the manufacturer's instructions.

If you liked this recipe, you will love these as well.

EGG CREAM ice cream

ZABAGLIONE ice cream

CINNAMON & MASCARPONE ice cream

EGG CREAM ice cream

Serves 6 • Preparation 30 minutes + 30 minutes to chill
+ time to churn • Difficulty 1

2	cups (500 ml) milk
2	cups (500 ml) heavy (double) cream
	Zest of 1/2 an organic lemon, in

	1 long piece, removed using a sharp knife
1 1/2	cups (300 g) sugar
8	large egg yolks

1. Combine the milk, cream, lemon zest, and 3/4 cup (150 g) of sugar in a heavy-based saucepan over medium heat and bring to a boil.

2. Beat the egg yolks and remaining sugar in a bowl with an electric mixer on high speed until pale and creamy.

3. Pour the hot milk mixture into the egg mixture, beating constantly. Return to the saucepan. Simmer over very low heat, stirring constantly, until it coats the back of a spoon. Do not let the mixture boil.

4. Pour into a bowl and let cool, stirring often. Chill in the refrigerator for 30 minutes.

5. Transfer the mixture to your ice cream machine and freeze following the manufacturer's instructions.

BOOZY VANILLA ice cream

Serves 4 • Preparation 25 minutes + 30 minutes to chill
+ time to churn • Difficulty 1

1	ounce (30 g) skim milk powder
1	cup (200 g) sugar
1/8	teaspoon salt
2	cups (500 ml) milk
1 2/3	cups (350 ml) heavy (double) cream

2	teaspoons vanilla extract (essence)
2/3	cup (180 ml) thick, creamy dessert liqueur, such Kahlua, Baileys Irish Cream, Drambuie, Grand Marnier, etc

1. Combine the milk powder, sugar, and salt in a heavy-based saucepan. Gradually stir in the milk and cream. Place the saucepan over medium heat and bring to a boil. Just before the mixture boils, turn the heat down to low and simmer for 2 minutes, stirring constantly.

2. Remove from the heat and stir in the vanilla extract. Let cool to room temperature. Chill in the refrigerator for 30 minutes.

3. Transfer the mixture to your ice cream machine and freeze following the manufacturer's instructions.

4. Scoop the ice cream into serving bowls or glasses and pour the liqueur over the top.

ZABAGLIONE ice cream

Serves 4 • Preparation 30 minutes + 30 minutes to chill
+ time to churn • Difficulty 1

1 2/3	cups (400 ml) milk
2/3	cup (150 ml) heavy (double) cream
4	large egg yolks
3/4	cup (150 g) sugar

1 1/2	tablespoons skim milk powder
1/3	cup (90 ml) Marsala wine + extra to serve (optional)

1. Combine the milk and cream in a heavy-based saucepan over medium heat and bring to a boil.

2. Beat the egg yolks, sugar, and skim milk powder in a medium bowl with an electric mixer on high speed until pale and creamy.

3. Pour the hot milk mixture into the egg mixture, beating constantly. Return to the saucepan. Simmer over very low heat, stirring constantly, until it coats the back of a spoon. Do not let the mixture boil.

4. Pour into a bowl and let cool, stirring often. Chill in the refrigerator for 30 minutes.

5. Transfer the mixture to your ice cream machine and freeze following the manufacturer's instructions.

6. Scoop into bowls and drizzle with (or drown in) extra Marsala wine, if desired.

LIME & GINGER ice cream

Serves 4 • Preparation 20 minutes + 30 minutes to chill
+ time to churn • Difficulty 1

4	large egg yolks
1	cup (150 g) sugar
1 1/2	teaspoons finely grated organic lime zest
1/3	cup (90 ml) milk
3	tablespoons candied

	(glacé) ginger, finely chopped
3/4	cup (180 ml) freshly squeezed lime juice
1 1/4	cups (300 g) mascarpone cheese

1. Beat the egg yolks, sugar, and lime zest in a small bowl with an electric mixer on high speed until pale and creamy.

2. Combine the milk and ginger in a small heavy-based saucepan over medium heat and bring to a boil. Gradually pour the milk mixture into the egg mixture, stirring constantly. Return to the pan and simmer over low heat, stirring constantly until it coats the back of a spoon. Do not allow the mixture to boil.

3. Pour into a bowl and let cool, stirring often. Chill in the refrigerator for 30 minutes.

4. Stir in the lime juice and mascarpone. Pour into your ice cream machine and churn according to the manufacturer's instructions.

CREAM CHEESE ice cream

1   cup (250 ml) light (single) cream
4   large egg yolks
3/4   cup (150 g) sugar
1 1/4 cups (300 g) cream cheese, softened
5   ounces (150 g) white chocolate, melted and cooled

Serves 4 • Preparation 20 minutes + 30 minutes to chill + time to churn
Cooking 5–10 minutes • Difficulty 1

1. Heat the cream in a heavy-based saucepan over medium heat and bring almost to a boil.

2. Beat the egg yolks and sugar in a medium bowl with an electric mixer on high speed until pale and creamy. Pour the hot cream into the egg mixture, stirring constantly.

3. Return to the saucepan and simmer over low heat, stirring constantly, until the custard coats the back of a spoon. Pour into a bowl and let cool, stirring often. Chill in the refrigerator for 30 minutes.

4. Beat the cream cheese with an electric mixer on medium speed until smooth. Pour in the white chocolate and the cooled custard and beat to combine.

5. Pour the mixture into your ice cream machine and churn according to the manufacturer's instructions.

NOUGAT ICE CREAM with cognac

2   cups (500 ml) milk

²/₃   cup (180 ml) heavy (double) cream

3   large egg yolks

³/₄   cup (150 g) sugar

1   tablespoon glucose

1   ounce (30 g) skim milk powder

¹/₄   cup (60 ml) cognac

4   ounces (120 g) crisp almond nougat, coarsely chopped

Serves 4 • Preparation 20 minutes + 30 minutes to chill + time to churn Cooking 5–10 minutes • Difficulty 1

1. Bring the milk and cream to a boil in a heavy-based saucepan over medium heat.

2. Beat the egg yolks and sugar in a medium bowl with an electric mixer on high speed until pale and creamy. Add the glucose and skim milk powder and beat until dissolved.

3. Pour the hot milk mixture into the egg yolk mixture, beating constantly. Return to the saucepan and simmer over very low heat, stirring constantly, until it just coats the back of a spoon. Do not let the mixture boil.

4. Pour into a bowl and let cool, stirring often. Chill in the refrigerator for 30 minutes. Whisk in the cognac.

5. Pour the mixture into your ice cream machine and churn according to the manufacturer's instructions. Add the nougat one minute before turning the machine off.

Cardamom is a fragrant, sweet spice native to southern India and Sri Lanka. Always use green cardamoms for flavoring dishes and try to buy the pods and either grind or infuse them to extract the flavor. Ground cardamom is also available but it quickly loses its flavor.

16

CARDAMOM ice cream

³/₄	cup (180 ml) milk
¹/₂	vanilla bean, split lengthwise
6	green cardamom pods, bruised
4	large egg yolks
¹/₂	cup (100 g) sugar
1²/₃	cups (400 ml) heavy (double) cream

Serves 4 • Preparation 30 minutes + 10 minutes to infuse + 30 minutes to chill + time to churn • Cooking 5–10 minutes • Difficulty 1

1. Combine the milk, vanilla bean, and cardamom pods in a small, heavy-based saucepan over medium heat and bring almost to a boil. Remove from the heat and set aside for 10 minutes for the vanilla and cardamom to infuse.

2. Beat the egg yolks and sugar in a medium bowl with an electric mixer on high speed until pale and creamy. Scrape the seeds from the vanilla bean into the milk and discard the bean. Pour the milk into the egg mixture, stirring constantly. Strain through a fine-mesh sieve.

3. Return to the saucepan and simmer over very low heat, stirring constantly, until the custard just coats the back of a spoon. Pour into a bowl and let cool, stirring often. Chill in the refrigerator for 30 minutes.

4. Stir in the cream then pour the mixture into your ice cream machine and churn according to the manufacturer's instructions.

If you liked this recipe, you will love these as well.

LIME & GINGER
ice cream

RUM & RAISIN
ice cream

WHISKY
ice cream

WALNUT ice cream

2 cups (500 ml) milk

2 cups (500 ml) heavy (double) cream

Zest of $1/2$ organic orange, in 1 long piece, removed using a sharp knife

1 cup (200 g) sugar

7 large egg yolks

1 teaspoon vanilla extract (essence)

1 cup (150 g) shelled walnuts, coarsely chopped

2 tablespoons rum

Wedges of aged pecorino cheese, to serve (optional)

Slices of fresh pear, to serve (optional)

Serves 6 • Preparation 30 minutes + 30 minutes to chill + time to churn
Cooking 5–10 minutes • Difficulty 1

1. Combine the milk, cream, orange zest, and $1/2$ cup (100 g) of sugar in a medium heavy-based saucepan over medium heat and bring to a boil. Remove from the heat and discard the orange zest.

2. Beat the egg yolks, remaining $1/2$ cup (100 g) sugar, and vanilla in a large bowl with an electric mixer on high speed until pale and creamy.

3. Pour the milk mixture into the egg yolk mixture, beating constantly. Return to the pan over very low heat and beat constantly until it just coats the back of a spoon. Do not let the mixture boil.

4. Pour into a bowl and let cool, stirring often. Stir in almost all the walnuts (reserve a few to garnish) and rum. Chill in the refrigerator for 30 minutes.

5. Transfer the mixture to your ice cream machine and churn according to the manufacturer's instructions.

6. Garnish the ice cream with the reserved walnuts and serve with the cheese and pears, if liked.

PEANUT BUTTER ice cream

1½ cups (375 ml) milk

1½ cups (375 ml) heavy
(double) cream

6 large egg yolks

½ cup (100 g) firmly packed
light brown sugar

1¼ cups (300 g) smooth peanut
butter

Serves 4–6 • Preparation 30 minutes + 30 minutes to chill + time to
churn • Cooking 5–10 minutes • Difficulty 1

1. Combine the milk and cream in a medium heavy-based
   saucepan over medium heat and bring almost to a boil.

2. Beat the egg yolks and brown sugar in a medium bowl
   with an electric mixer on high speed until creamy. Pour the
   milk mixture into the egg mixture, stirring constantly.

3. Return the custard to the saucepan and simmer over very
   low heat, stirring constantly, until it just coats the back of
   a spoon.

4. Pour into a bowl and let cool, stirring often. Stir in the
   peanut butter and chill in the refrigerator for 30 minutes.

5. Transfer the mixture to your ice cream machine and churn
   according to the manufacturer's instructions.

Rum and raisin is a classic ice cream flavor. If preferred, use rum-flavored extract (essence), instead of real rum; you will need about 1 tablespoon of rum extract.

RUM & RAISIN ice cream

½   cup (90 g) raisins
6   tablespoons (90 ml) dark rum
1¼   cups (300 ml) light (single) cream
4   large egg yolks
½   cup (100 g) firmly packed light brown sugar
¾   cup (180 ml) heavy (double) cream

Serves 4 • Preparation 15 minutes + overnight to soak + 30 minutes to chill + time to churn • Cooking 5–10 minutes • Level: 1

1. Plump the raisins in 4 tablespoons (60 ml) of rum in a small bowl overnight.

2. Heat the light cream in a small saucepan over medium heat until almost boiling.

3. Beat the egg yolks and brown sugar with an electric mixer on high speed in a medium bowl until creamy. Pour the hot milk mixture into the egg mixture. Return to the saucepan over very low heat, stirring constantly, until thick enough to coat the back of a spoon.

4. Pour into a bowl and let cool, stirring often. Chill in the refrigerator for 30 minutes.

5. Stir in the heavy cream and remaining 2 tablespoons of rum. Transfer to your ice cream machine and churn according to the manufacturer's instructions until almost completely frozen. Add the raisins and churn until just combined, about 2 minutes.

If you liked this recipe, you will love these as well.

RAISIN & ROSEMARY
ice cream

CHOCOLATE HAZELNUT
ice cream

ROCKY ROAD
ice cream

RAISIN & ROSEMARY ice cream

1³/₄ cups (450 ml) milk

3 tablespoons fresh rosemary leaves

³/₄ cup (150 g) sugar

1²/₃ cups (400 ml) heavy (double) cream

¹/₈ teaspoon salt

2 tablespoons best-quality extra-virgin olive oil

2 ounces (60 g) Corinth raisins

Serves 4–6 • Preparation 20 minutes + 1 hour to infuse + 30 minutes to chill + time to churn • Cooking 15 minutes • Difficulty 1

1. Combine the milk and rosemary in a heavy-based saucepan over medium heat and bring to a boil. Remove from the heat and let infuse for 1 hour. Strain through a fine-mesh sieve, discarding the rosemary.

2. Combine the sugar, infused milk, cream, and salt in a heavy-bottomed saucepan over medium heat and bring to a boil. Decrease the heat to low and simmer for 2 minutes, stirring constantly. Remove from the heat and stir in the oil.

3. Beat with an electric mixer on low speed until cool. Chill in the refrigerator for 30 minutes.

4. Beat with a whisk for 2–3 minutes. Transfer the mixture to an ice-cream maker and churn according to the manufacturer's instructions.

5. Serve the ice cream sprinkled with the raisins.

CINNAMON & MASCARPONE ice cream

1 cup (200 g) firmly packed light brown sugar
1⅓ cups (330 ml) water
1 cinnamon stick
1⅔ cups (400 g) mascarpone
⅔ cup (160 ml) heavy (double) cream

Serves 4 • Preparation 20 minutes + 30 minutes to chill • Cooking 10 minutes • Difficulty 1

1. Combine the sugar, water, and cinnamon in a medium saucepan over medium-high heat and bring to a boil. Decrease the heat to low and simmer for 10 minutes.

2. Pour into a medium bowl and let cool. Chill in the refrigerator for 30 minutes.

3. Discard the cinnamon stick. Stir the mascarpone and cream into the sugar syrup. Transfer to an ice cream machine and churn according to the manufacturer's instructions.

This recipe comes from Piedmont, in Italy, where the flavor is known as *gianduia*. Chocolate hazelnut cream is used not only to flavor ice cream, but also to fill cakes and pies, and as a spread for bread.

CHOCOLATE HAZELNUT ice cream

$^1/_2$	cup (60 g) toasted (unsalted) hazelnuts + extra to garnish
4	tablespoons confectioners' (icing) sugar
4	ounces (120 g) dark chocolate
$2^1/_3$	cups (600 ml) milk
$^1/_2$	cup (125 ml) heavy (double) cream
4	large egg yolks
$^3/_4$	cup (150 g) sugar

Serves 4 • Preparation 20 minutes + 30 minutes to chill + time to churn
Cooking 10–15 minutes • Difficulty 1

1. Chop the hazelnuts and confectioners' sugar in a food processor until smooth. Melt the chocolate in a double boiler over barely simmering water. Stir the chocolate into the hazelnut mixture and set aside.

2. Combine the milk and cream in a heavy-based saucepan over medium heat and bring to a boil.

3. Beat the egg yolks and sugar in a medium bowl with an electric mixer on high speed until pale and creamy. Pour the milk mixture into the egg mixture, beating constantly. Return to the saucepan and simmer over very low heat, stirring constantly, until the mixture just coats the back of the spoon. Do not let it boil.

4. Stir a little of the hot milk mixture into the chocolate mixture. Pour the chocolate mixture into the hot milk. Beat until cool. Chill in the refrigerator for 30 minutes.

5. Transfer the mixture to your ice cream machine and churn according to the manufacturer's instructions

If you liked this recipe, you will love these as well.

MOCHA
ice cream

CHOCOLATE ORANGE
ice cream

DOUBLE CHOCOLATE CHIP ice cream

COFFEE ice cream

2 cups (500 ml) milk
2 tablespoons instant coffee granules
2 cups (500 ml) heavy (double) cream
2 teaspoons vanilla extract (essence)
6 large egg yolks
1¼ cups (250 g) sugar
Coffee beans, to serve
Whipped cream, to serve

Serves 6 • Preparation 20 minutes + 30 minutes to chill + time to churn • Cooking: 5-10 minutes • Difficulty 1

1. Combine the milk and coffee in a heavy-based saucepan over medium heat and bring to a boil. Remove from the heat and stir in the cream and vanilla.

2. Beat the egg yolks and sugar in a bowl with an electric mixer on high speed until pale and creamy. Pour the hot milk mixture into the egg mixture, beating constantly. Return the mixture to the saucepan over very low heat and simmer, stirring constantly, until it just coats the back of the spoon. Do not let the mixture boil.

3. Pour into a bowl and let cool, stirring often. Chill in the refrigerator for 30 minutes.

4. Transfer the mixture to your ice cream machine and churn according to the manufacturer's instructions.

5. Serve in bowls or glasses topped with the whipped cream and coffee beans.

MOCHA ice cream

- 2 ounces (60 g) coffee beans, coarsely ground
- 2¼ cups (550 ml) milk + extra, as required
- 4 large egg yolks
- ¾ cup (150 g) sugar
- 1 tablespoon powdered glucose
- 1 ounce (30 g) unsweetened cocoa powder, sifted
- ⅔ cup (180 ml) heavy (double) cream

Serves 4 • Preparation 30 minutes + 30 minutes to chill + time to churn
Cooking 10–15 minutes • Difficulty 1

1. Combine the coffee and milk in a heavy-based saucepan over medium heat and bring to a boil. Simmer for 2 minutes then strain through a fine-mesh sieve. Measure again to make sure you still have 2¼ cups (550 ml) of milk. Add more milk if necessary.

2. Combine the milk mixture and cream in a heavy-based saucepan over medium heat and bring to a boil.

3. Beat the egg yolks and sugar in a medium bowl with an electric mixer on high speed until pale and creamy. Add the glucose and beat until dissolved.

4. Pour the hot milk mixture into the egg mixture, beating constantly. Return to the saucepan and simmer over very low heat, stirring constantly, until it just coats the back of the spoon. Do not let the mixture boil.

5. Place the cocoa in a bowl and add a little of the milk mixture, stirring until smooth. Add the remaining milk mixture and the cream. Let cool, stirring often. Refrigerate for 30 minutes.

6. Transfer the mixture to your ice cream machine and churn according to the manufacturer's instructions.

Serve this ice cream with hot apple pie or crumble, or scooped into bowls on its own drizzled with extra whisky.

WHISKY ice cream

1½ cups (625 ml) milk
6 large egg yolks
4 tablespoons sugar
⅓ cup (80 ml) honey
2 tablespoons whisky + extra to serve
¼ teaspoon ground cinnamon
½ cup (125 ml) heavy (double) cream

Serves 4 • Preparation 30 minutes + 30 minutes to chill + time to churn
Cooking 5–10 minutes • Difficulty 1

1. Put the milk in a small heavy-based saucepan over medium heat and bring to a boil. Remove from the heat.

2. Beat the egg yolks and sugar in a medium bowl with an electric mixer on high speed until pale and creamy. Pour in the hot milk, stirring to combine. Return the mixture to the saucepan and simmer over very low heat, stirring constantly, until it coats the back of the spoon. Stir in the honey, whisky, cinnamon and heavy cream.

3. Pour into a bowl and let cool. Chill in the refrigerator for 30 minutes.

4. Transfer to your ice cream machine and churn according to the manufacturer's instructions.

5. Scoop the ice cream into four serving glasses. Drizzle with (or drown in) extra whisky to taste and serve.

If you liked this recipe, you will love these as well.

BOOZY VANILLA ice cream

RUM & RAISIN ice cream

ICE CREAM with port & almond biscotti

COCONUT ICE CREAM with sesame tuiles

Coconut Ice Cream

$^{1}/_{2}$ cup (100 g) sugar

$^{1}/_{2}$ cup (100 g) grated jaggery (palm sugar)

$^{3}/_{4}$ cup (180 ml) water

$1^{1}/_{3}$ cups (400 ml) coconut milk

1 cup (250 ml) heavy (double) cream

Shredded coconut or coconut curls to garnish

Black Sesame Tuiles

1 large egg white, lightly beaten with a fork

3 tablespoons superfine (caster) sugar

$1^{1}/_{2}$ teaspoons all-purpose (plain) flour

3 tablespoons black sesame seeds

2 teaspoons cold-pressed light sesame oil

Serves 4 • Preparation 45 minutes + 1 hour to rest + 30 minutes to chill + time to churn • Cooking 15-20 minutes • Difficulty 3

Coconut Ice Cream

1. Combine the sugar, jaggery, and water in a medium saucepan over medium and bring to a boil. Remove from the heat and stir in the coconut milk and cream. Chill in the refrigerator for 30 minutes. Pour into an ice cream machine and churn according to the manufacturer's instructions.

Black Sesame Tuiles

1. Put the egg white in a small bowl. Add the sugar, flour, sesame seeds, and sesame oil and whisk until combined. Cover with plastic wrap and let rest for 1 hour.

2. Preheat the oven to 425°F (220°C/gas 7). Line two cookie sheets with parchment paper. Trace $2^{1}/_{2}$-inch (6-cm) circles onto the parchment paper with a pencil (use a small coffee cup or an egg cup), leaving $^{1}/_{2}$ inch (1 cm) between each one. Place $^{3}/_{4}$ teaspoon of tuile mixture in each circle and spread with a palette knife. You will get about 20 tuiles.

3. Have two rolling pins handy for shaping the cookies. Bake, one sheet at a time, for 5 minutes, or until the tuiles are golden. Working quickly, lay the tuiles over the rolling pins to shape. Slip off and let cool and harden. Serve with the ice cream.

YOGURT ice cream

- $3/4$ cup (150 g) sugar
- 1 ounce (30 g) skim milk powder
- $2/3$ tablespoon powdered glucose
- $1^3/4$ cups (450 g) plain yogurt
- $3/4$ cup (200 ml) heavy (double) cream
- $2/3$ cup (180 ml) milk

Serves 4 • Preparation 20 minutes + 30 minutes to chill + time to churn
Cooking 2–3 minutes • Difficulty 1

1. Combine the sugar, skim milk powder, and glucose in a heavy-based saucepan. Stir in the yogurt, cream, and milk. Place over medium-high heat and bring to a boil. As soon as the mixture boils, turn the heat down to low and simmer for 2–3 minutes, stirring constantly.

2. Remove from the heat and pour into a bowl. Beat with a whisk until cool. Chill in the refrigerator for 30 minutes.

3. Beat with a whisk for 2–3 minutes. Transfer the mixture to your ice cream machine and churn according to the manufacturer's instructions.

Chocolate and orange are a classic taste combination. Serve this ice cream scooped into dessert bowls or glasses. The recipe makes use of the orange peel; if liked, slice the leftover oranges and serve with the ice cream.

CHOCOLATE ORANGE ice cream

2	ounces (60 g) unsweetened cocoa powder, sifted
2	small organic oranges
2¼	cups (550 ml) milk
⅔	cup (180 ml) heavy (double) cream
1	tablespoon glucose
1	ounce (30 g) skim milk powder
3	large egg yolks
¾	cup (150 g) sugar
⅛	teaspoon salt
3	ounces (90 g) candied (glacé) orange, cut in tiny cubes

Serves 4 • Preparation 20 minutes + 30 minutes to chill + time to churn
Cooking 5 minutes • Difficulty 1

1. Put the cocoa in a medium bowl. Peel the oranges with a sharp knife, removing every trace of the bitter white inner peel from the orange outer peel.

2. Combine the milk, cream, and orange peel in a heavy-based saucepan over medium heat and bring to a boil. Remove from the heat and let rest for 30 minutes. Strain through a fine-mesh sieve. Add the glucose and milk powder and stir until dissolved.

3. Beat the egg yolks, sugar, and salt in a medium bowl with an electric mixer on high speed until pale and creamy.

4. Pour the milk mixture into the egg yolk mixture, stirring constantly. Return to the saucepan over very low heat and stir constantly until the mixture just coats the back of the spoon. Do not let the mixture boil.

5. Pour a little of the hot milk mixture into the bowl with the cocoa, stirring until smooth. Stir in the rest of the milk mixture. Transfer to a bowl and let cool, stirring often. Chill in the refrigerator for 30 minutes.

6. Transfer the mixture to your ice cream machine and churn according to the manufacturer's instructions. Add the candied orange one minute before the ice cream is ready.

RICE CREAM with chocolate sauce

Rice Cream

2	cups (500 ml) milk
³/₄	cup (150 g) short-grain or pudding rice
1	vanilla pod, slit open lengthwise
	Generous ¹/₄ cup (50 g) golden raisins (sultanas)
¹/₄	teaspoon salt
	Finely grated zest of 1 organic orange
	Finely grated zest and juice of 1 organic lemon
2	tablespoons honey or brown rice syrup

Chocolate Sauce

8	ounces (250 g) dark chocolate, grated
1¹/₂	cups (375 ml) milk
2	scant teaspoons cornstarch (cornflour)
¹/₂	cup (50 g) superfine (caster) sugar

Serves 4 • Preparation 15 minutes + 30 minutes to cool + time to churn
Cooking 25 minutes • Difficulty 2

Rice Cream

1. Combine the milk, rice, vanilla pod, and golden raisins in a heavy-based saucepan over medium heat. Bring to a boil, then decrease the heat to low. Stir in the salt. Simmer, stirring constantly, until the rice is tender and has absorbed almost all the milk, about 15 minutes. Remove from the heat and discard the vanilla pod. Let cool, stirring often.

2. Stir in the orange zest, lemon zest, lemon juice, and honey. Transfer the mixture to an ice cream machine and churn according to the manufacturer's instructions.

Chocolate Sauce

1. Combine the chocolate and ³/₄ cup (200 ml) of milk in a saucepan over medium heat and bring to a boil. Dissolve the cornstarch in the remaining milk and mix into the chocolate along with the sugar. Stir over low heat until the sugar is dissolved. Whisk until smooth.

2. Scoop the ice cream into serving dishes and drizzle with the warm chocolate sauce.

ROCKY ROAD ice cream

- 2 cups (500 ml) milk
- 2 cups (500 ml) heavy (double) cream
- 8 ounces (250 g) dark chocolate, coarsely chopped
- 4 large egg yolks
- ½ cup (100 g) superfine (caster) sugar
- ¼ cup (30 g) unsweetened cocoa powder
- ¼ cup (40 g) roasted peanuts
- ¼ cup (45 g) candied (glacé) cherries
- ¼ cup mini marshmallows
- 2 tablespoons shredded coconut

Serves 4–6 • Preparation 20 minutes + 30 minutes to cool + time to churn • Cooking 15 minutes • Difficulty 2

1. Heat the milk and cream in a heavy-based saucepan over medium heat. Bring almost to a boil, then remove from the heat. Put the chocolate in a heatproof bowl and pour in half the hot milk mixture, stirring until melted.

2. Beat the egg yolks, sugar, and cocoa in a medium bowl with an electric mixer until creamy. Pour in the remaining milk mixture and the chocolate mixture, whisking to combine.

3. Return to the saucepan and simmer over low heat, stirring constantly, until the mixture coats the back of the spoon. Remove from the heat and let cool, about 30 minutes.

4. Pour the custard mixture into your ice cream machine and churn according to the manufacturer's instructions until almost frozen. Add the peanuts, candied cherries, marshmallows, and coconut and churn until incorporated, about 3 minutes.

CHOCOLATE CHIP ice cream

Serves 4–6 • Preparation 30 minutes + 30 minutes to chill + time to churn • Cooking 5–10 minutes • Difficulty 1

2	cups (500 ml) milk	1½	cups (300 g) sugar
2	cups (500 ml) heavy (double) cream	8	large egg yolks
1	teaspoon vanilla extract (essence)	4	ounces (125 g) dark chocolate, melted
		2	tablespoons rum

1. Combine the milk, cream, vanilla, and ¾ cup (150 g) of sugar in a heavy-based saucepan over medium heat and bring to a boil.

2. Beat the egg yolks and remaining sugar in a large bowl with an electric mixer at high speed until pale and creamy.

3. Pour the hot milk mixture into the egg mixture, stirring constantly. Return to the saucepan and simmer over very low heat, stirring constantly, until it just coats the back of the spoon. Do not let it boil.

4. Pour into a bowl and let cool, stirring often. Chill in the refrigerator for 30 minutes.

5. Transfer to your ice cream machine and churn according to the manufacturer's instructions. Add the chocolate and rum 1–2 minutes before the ice cream is ready.

CHOCOLATE ICE CREAM with fresh mint

Serves 4 • Preparation 30 minutes + 30 minutes to chill + time to churn • Cooking 5–10 minutes • Difficulty 1

2	cups (500 ml) milk	4	tablespoons unsweetened cocoa powder
1	cup (250 ml) heavy (double) cream		Fresh mint leaves, to serve
4	large egg yolks		
1	cup (200 g) sugar		

1. Combine the milk and cream in a heavy-based saucepan over medium heat and bring to a boil.

2. Beat the egg yolks and sugar in with an electric mixer on high speed until pale and creamy. Beat in the cocoa.

3. Pour the hot milk mixture into the egg mixture, stirring constantly. Return to the saucepan over very low heat and simmer, stirring constantly with a wooden spoon, until it coats the back of the spoon.

4. Pour into a bowl and let cool, stirring often. Chill in the refrigerator for 30 minutes.

5. Transfer to your ice cream machine and churn according to the manufacturer's instructions.

6. Scoop into serving glasses or bowls and decorate with the fresh mint leaves.

DOUBLE CHOCOLATE CHIP ice cream

Serves 4–6 • Preparation 30 minutes + 30 minutes to chill + time to churn • Cooking 5–10 minutes • Difficulty 1

8	ounces (250 g) dark chocolate, chopped	2	cups (500 ml) heavy (double) cream
6	large egg yolks	1	cup (250 ml) milk
½	cup (100 g) sugar	5	ounces (150 g) dark chocolate chips

1. Put the chocolate in a large bowl and set aside. Beat the egg yolks and sugar with an electric mixer at high speed until pale and creamy.

2. Bring the cream and milk to a boil in a saucepan over medium heat. Pour half the hot cream mixture into the egg mixture, beating constantly. Return to the pan with the remaining cream mixture and return to low heat. Stir constantly until it coats the back of the spoon.

3. Pour over the chocolate and stir until melted. Chill in the refrigerator for 30 minutes. Stir in the chocolate chips.

4. Transfer to an ice cream machine and churn according to the manufacturers instructions.

MINTY CHOCOLATE CHIP ice cream

Serves 4–6 • Preparation 30 minutes + 30 minutes to chill + time to churn • Cooking 5–10 minutes • Difficulty 1

2	cups (500 ml) light (single) cream	5	ounces (150 g) dark chocolate, coarsely grated
1	cup (250 ml) milk	¼	teaspoon mint extract (essence)
6	large egg yolks		
½	cup (100 g) sugar		

1. Combine the cream and milk in a heavy-based saucepan over medium heat and bring to a boil.

2. Beat the egg yolks and sugar with an electric mixer on high speed until pale and creamy.

3. Pour the hot milk mixture into the egg mixture, stirring constantly. Return to the saucepan over very low heat and simmer, stirring constantly with a wooden spoon, until it coats the back of the spoon.

4. Pour into a bowl and let cool, stirring often. Chill in the refrigerator for 30 minutes. Add the chocolate and peppermint extract.

5. Transfer to your ice cream machine and churn according to the manufacturer's instructions.

Amarena cherries are delicious, slightly tart cherries that grow in the Emilia-Romagna region of central Italy. They are available in cans or jars in Italian food stores. If you can't find them, replace with sour cherries or a good quality, highly flavored local cherry.

AMARENA CHERRY ice cream

1	ounce (30 g) skim milk powder
$3/4$	cup (150 g) sugar
$1^3/4$	cups (450 ml) milk
$1^1/3$	cups (300 ml) heavy (double) cream
$1/8$	teaspoon salt
2	tablespoons amarena cherry syrup
4	ounces (120 g) canned amarena cherries (drained weight)
	Fresh cherries to decorate (optional)

Serves 4 • Preparation 20 minutes + 30 minutes to chill + time to churn • Cooking 2-3 minutes • Difficulty 1

1. Mix the skim milk powder and sugar in a heavy-based saucepan and then add the milk, cream, and salt. Place over medium heat and, just before the mixture begins to boil, turn the heat down to low and simmer for 2-3 minutes, stirring constantly.

2. Remove from the heat, add the amarena cherry syrup, and beat with a whisk on medium speed until cool. Chill in the refrigerator for 30 minutes.

3. Beat with a whisk for 2-3 minutes. Transfer the mixture to your ice cream machine and churn according to the manufacturer's instructions.

4. Cut the amarena cherries in half and add them to the ice cream machine one minute before you turn it off. Decorate with the whole fresh cherries, if desired.

If you liked this recipe, you will love these as well.

TURKISH DELIGHT
ice cream

CHERRY BRANDY
sorbet

BLACKBERRY
sorbet

TURKISH DELIGHT ice cream

1¼ cups (300 ml) heavy (double) cream
1 cup (250 ml) milk
6 large egg yolks
⅓ cup (70 g) sugar
1 teaspoon rose water
4 ounces (120 g) Turkish delight, coarsely diced

Serves 4 • Preparation 20 minutes + 30 minutes to chill + time to churn • Cooking 5 minutes • Difficulty 1

1. Combine the cream and milk in a medium, heavy-based saucepan over medium heat and bring to a boil.

2. Beat the egg yolks, sugar, and rose water in a medium bowl with an electric mixer on high speed until pale and creamy.

3. Pour the hot cream mixture into the egg yolk mixture, stirring constantly. Return the mixture to the saucepan over low heat and simmer, stirring constantly, until it coats the back of the spoon. Do not allow the mixture to boil.

4. Pour into a bowl and let cool. Chill in the refrigerator for 30 minutes. Stir in the Turkish delight.

5. Transfer to your ice cream machine and churn according to the manufacturer's instructions.

ICE CREAM with port & almond biscotti

2   cups (500 ml) milk
$^3/_4$ cup (200 ml) heavy (double) cream
6   large egg yolks
$^3/_4$ cup (150 g) sugar
5   tablespoons (75 ml) port (or sherry)
20   Italian almond biscotti, coarsely chopped

Serves 4-6 • Preparation 20 minutes + 30 minutes to cool + time to churn • Cooking 5 minutes • Difficulty 1

1. Combine the milk and cream in a medium, heavy-based saucepan over medium heat and bring to a boil.

2. Beat the egg yolks and sugar in a medium bowl with an electric mixer on high speed until pale and creamy.

3. Pour the hot cream mixture into the egg yolk mixture, stirring constantly. Return the mixture to the saucepan over low heat and simmer, stirring constantly, until it coats the back of the spoon. Do not allow the mixture to boil.

4. Pour into a bowl and let cool. Chill in the refrigerator for 30 minutes. Stir in the port. Transfer to your ice cream machine and churn according to the manufacturer's instructions.

5. Divide three-quarters of the biscotti evenly among four to six serving glasses or bowls and top with the ice cream. Sprinkle with the remaining biscotti and serve.

You can make a superb lime ice cream by replacing the mandarin juice in this recipe with the same quantity of freshly squeezed lime juice. Increase the amount of sugar to 1 cup (200 g).

42

CREAM OF MANDARIN ice cream

1	cup (250 ml) heavy (double) cream
$2^1/_3$	cups (600 ml) freshly squeezed mandarin juice (about 15 mandarins)
3	large egg yolks
$^2/_3$	cup (130 g) sugar
2	tablespoons (30 ml) mandarin liqueur (optional)

Serves 4 • Preparation 20 minutes + 30 minutes to cool + time to churn • Cooking 5 minutes • Difficulty 1

1. Place the cream in a heavy-based saucepan over medium heat and bring to a boil.

2. Beat the egg yolks and sugar in a medium bowl with an electric mixer on high speed until pale and creamy.

3. Pour the hot cream into the egg mixture, stirring constantly with a wooden spoon. Return the mixture to the saucepan. Simmer over very low heat, stirring constantly, until it just coats the back of the spoon. Do not let the mixture boil.

4. Pour into a bowl and let cool, stirring often. Stir in the mandarin juice and liqueur, if using, and chill in the refrigerator for 30 minutes.

5. Transfer the mixture to your ice cream machine and churn according to the manufacturer's instructions.

If you liked this recipe, you will love these as well.

LEMON
ice cream

ORANGE
sorbet

LEMON
granita

BANANA ice cream

1¼ cups (300 ml) heavy (double) cream
1 cup (250 ml) milk
1 teaspoon ground nutmeg
6 large egg yolks
⅓ cup (70 g) sugar
3 large ripe bananas, mashed
3 tablespoons honey

Serves 4 • Preparation 20 minutes + 30 minutes to chill + time to churn • Cooking 5 minutes • Difficulty 1

1. Combine the cream, milk, and nutmeg in a medium, heavy-based saucepan over medium heat and bring to a boil.

2. Beat the egg yolks and sugar in a medium bowl with an electric mixer on high speed until pale and creamy. Stir in the bananas and honey.

3. Pour the hot cream mixture into the egg yolk mixture, stirring constantly. Return to the pan and simmer over very low heat, stirring constantly, until the mixture coats the back of the spoon. Do not allow it to boil.

4. Pour into a bowl and let cool. Chill in the refrigerator for 30 minutes.

5. Transfer the mixture to your ice cream machine and churn according to the manufacturer's instructions.

LEMON ice cream

8 organic lemons, unblemished and of even size

1³/₄ cups (350 g) sugar

1 cup (250 ml) water

¹/₈ teaspoon salt

³/₄ cup (200 ml) milk

2 large egg whites

Finely grated organic lemon zest, to garnish (optional)

Serves 4 • Preparation 20 minutes + 30 minutes to cool + time to churn Cooking 5 minutes • Difficulty 1

1. Cut the top third off the lemons and scoop out the flesh with a teaspoon. Place in a bowl lined with muslin. Arrange lemon skins on a large tray and place in the freezer.

2. Wrap the lemon flesh in the muslin and squeeze the juice into the bowl. You should get ³/₄ cup (200 ml) of juice.

3. Heat 1¹/₄ cups (250 g) of sugar with the water and salt in a large heavy-based saucepan over low heat. Stir until the sugar has dissolved, 3–4 minutes. Remove from the heat and add the milk and lemon juice. Mix well and let cool.

4. Beat the egg whites in a large bowl with an electric mixer on high speed until soft peaks form. Add the remaining sugar and beat until stiff. Fold into the lemon mixture.

5. Transfer the mixture to your ice cream machine and churn according to the manufacturer's instructions.

6. When the ice cream is frozen, spoon it into the frozen lemon skins. Store in the freezer until ready to serve. If liked, garnish with grated lemon zest.

BITTER CHOCOLATE sorbet

2¹/₂ cups (625 ml) water

1¹/₂ cups (250 g) sugar

2¹/₂ teaspoons instant coffee granules

¹/₃ cup (50 g) unsweetened cocoa powder, sifted

3¹/₂ ounces (100 g) good-quality bittersweet or dark (at least 70% cacao) chocolate

Serves 4 • Preparation: 15 minutes + 2 hours to chill + time to churn
Cooking 5 minutes • Difficulty 1

1. Combine the water, sugar, coffee, cocoa powder, and chocolate in a medium saucepan over medium heat and bring to a boil. Simmer over very low heat for 5 minutes.

2. Remove from the heat and strain through a fine-mesh sieve into a bowl. Chill in the refrigerator for 2 hours.

3. Pour the mixture into an ice-cream maker and churn according to the manufacturer's instructions.

If you liked this recipe, you will love these as well.

DOUBLE CHOCOLATE CHIP ice cream

CHOCOLATE ICE CREAM with fresh mint

CHOCOLATE MINT sorbet

Ice creams, sorbets, and granitas can be made ahead of time. If you are not serving them immediately, transfer them to a freezer container, cover with parchment paper, and freeze until you are ready to serve. If storing for more than just a few hours, be sure to seal the container with a lid as they can absorb other odors from the freezer, spoiling their delicious homemade flavors.

ORANGE sorbet

1¼   cups (250 g) sugar
1   cup (250 ml) water
3   juicy oranges
1   tablespoon Grand Marnier or other orange-flavored liqueur
      Fresh mint leaves, to garnish

Serves 4 • Preparation: 30 minutes + 2 hours to chill + time to churn
Cooking 2–3 minutes • Difficulty 1

1. Combine the sugar and water in a medium saucepan over medium heat and bring to a boil, stirring often, until the sugar has dissolved, 2–3 minutes.

2. Cut the oranges in half crosswise. Squeeze out 1¼ cups (300 ml) of juice. Reserve the skins. Add the orange juice and Grand Marnier to the sugar mixture. Strain through a fine-mesh sieve into a bowl and set aside to cool. Chill in the refrigerator for two hours.

3. Scrape out any remaining flesh from the orange skins with a spoon. Reserve the four best-looking halves and trim the bottoms, if necessary, so that they stand flat. Place the orange skins in the freezer until you are ready to serve.

4. Pour the chilled orange mixture into your ice cream machine and churn according to the manufacturer's instructions.

5. Place the frozen orange skins on individual serving plates. Fill with the sorbet and garnish with mint.

If you liked this recipe, you will love these as well.

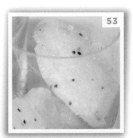

KIWI sorbet

RASPBERRY sorbet

LEMON SORBET
with strawberries

CHERRY BRANDY sorbet

Serves 2-4 • Preparation 15 minutes + 30 minutes to chill + time to churn • Cooking 2-3 minutes • Difficulty 1

1¼	cups (300 ml) water	⅔	cup (180 ml) kirsch (cherry brandy)
¼	cup (50 g) sugar		Fresh cherries, to garnish
2	cloves		
½	cinnamon stick		

1. Combine the water, sugar, cloves, and cinnamon in a saucepan over medium heat. Bring to a boil and simmer, stirring often, until the sugar has dissolved, 2-3 minutes.

2. Remove from the heat and strain through a fine-mesh sieve into a large bowl. Chill in the refrigerator for 30 minutes, then stir in the kirsch.

3. Transfer the mixture to your ice cream machine and churn according to the manufacturer's instructions.

4. Spoon or pipe the sorbet into serving bowls or glasses. Garnish with the cherries.

BLUE CURAÇAO sorbet

Serves 4 • Preparation 15 minutes + 30 minutes to chill + time to churn • Cooking 2-3 minutes • Difficulty 2

¾	cup (150 g) sugar	¾	cup (200 ml) heavy (double) cream
¾	cup (200 ml) water	⅔	cup (180 ml) blue curaçao
1	cup (250 ml) white port		Fresh cherries, to garnish (optional)
	Freshly squeezed juice of 1 lemon		

1. Combine the sugar and water in a medium saucepan over medium heat and bring to a boil. Simmer, stirring often, until the sugar has dissolved, 2-3 minutes. Set aside and let cool.

2. Pour into a large bowl. Chill in the refrigerator for 30 minutes. Stir in the port and lemon juice.

3. Transfer the mixture to your ice cream machine and churn according to the manufacturer's instructions.

4. Beat the cream with an electric mixer on high speed until thick. Fold the blue curaçao into the cream. Fold the blue cream into the cooled sugar syrup. Spoon or pipe into serving bowls or glasses and garnish with a cherry.

WILLIAMS PEAR sorbet

Serves 4 • Preparation 20 minutes + 30 minutes to cool + time to churn • Cooking 2-3 minutes • Difficulty 1

1¾	cups (350 g) sugar		Freshly squeezed juice of ½ lemon
1⅔	cups (400 ml) water	⅓	cup (90 ml) Williams pear liqueur
2	pounds (1 kg) ripe Williams pears		

1. Combine the sugar and water in a saucepan over medium heat. Bring to a boil and simmer, stirring often, until the sugar has dissolved, 2-3 minutes. Set aside to cool for 30 minutes.

2. Peel and core the pears. Reserve a few slices to garnish. Transfer the remaining pears to a food processor and add the lemon juice. Blend to make a smooth purée.

3. Stir the pear purée and liqueur into the cooled sugar syrup. Transfer to your ice cream machine and churn according to the manufacturer's instructions.

4. Spoon or pipe the sorbet into serving bowls or glasses and garnish with the slices of pear.

AFTER DINNER sorbet

Serves 4 • Preparation 15 minutes + 30 minutes to cool + time to churn • Cooking 2-3 minutes • Difficulty 1

¾	cup (150 g) sugar		of 1 orange
¾	cup (200 ml) water	¾	cup (200 ml) heavy (double) cream
1	cup (250 ml) white port	⅔	cup (180 ml) single malt whisky
	Freshly squeezed juice		

1. Combine the sugar and water in a saucepan over medium heat and bring to a boil. Simmer, stirring often, until the sugar has dissolved, 2-3 minutes. Set aside to cool for 30 minutes.

2. Stir the port and orange juice into the cooled sugar syrup. Transfer to your ice cream machine and churn according to the manufacturer's instructions.

3. Beat the cream in a small bowl with an electric mixer on high speed until thick. When the sorbet is almost ready, add the cream and ⅓ cup (90 ml) of whisky and let the machine finish churning.

4. Spoon or pipe the sorbet into serving glasses and top each one with a little of the remaining whisky.

MELON sorbet

1 pound (500 g) cantaloupe
(rock) melon flesh, peeled
weight, cut in cubes

6 fresh basil leaves + extra to
garnish

1/3 cup (90 ml) freshly squeezed
orange juice

3/4 cup (150 g) superfine (caster)
sugar

1/4 teaspoon salt

Serves 4 • Preparation 15 minutes + 1 hour to chill + time to churn
Difficulty 1

1. Combine the melon cubes and basil in a blender with the
orange juice, sugar, and salt. Chop until the sugar has
dissolved and the mixture is smooth, about 30 seconds.

2. Transfer to a bowl and chill in the refrigerator for 1 hour.

3. Transfer to your ice cream machine and churn according
to the manufacturer's instructions.

4. Spoon or pipe the sorbet into serving glasses. Garnish
with the extra basil leaves.

KIWI sorbet

1   cup (200 g) sugar
1¼   cups (300 ml) water
6   ripe kiwi fruit, peeled
1   tablespoon Cointreau
       Slices of mandarin, cut in half
       to garnish

Serves 4 • Preparation 15 minutes + 30 minutes to cool + time to churn
Cooking 2–3 minutes • Difficulty 1

1. Combine the sugar and $^3/_4$ cup (200 ml) of water in a medium saucepan over medium heat and bring to a boil. Simmer, stirring often, until the sugar has dissolved, 2–3 minutes. Set aside to cool for 30 minutes.

2. Chop the kiwi fruit in a food processor until smooth. Press through a fine-mesh strainer to remove the seeds.

3. Weigh out $^2/_3$ cup (180 g) of the purée and stir it into the sugar syrup. Stir in the Cointreau and remaining water.

4. Transfer to your ice cream machine and churn according to the manufacturer's instructions.

5. Spoon or pipe the sorbet into serving glasses. Garnish with the mandarin.

A sorbet is a water ice based on a sugar syrup. It is usually flavored with fruit juice or purée, or a wine or liqueur. Strictly speaking, sorbets do not contain milk products, but in this recipe we have added a little yogurt to mellow the flavor of the fruit.

STRAWBERRY YOGURT sorbet

$^1/_2$ cup (100 g) sugar
2   cups (500 ml) water
3   cups (450 g) fresh
    strawberries
$1^1/_4$ cups (300 g) plain yogurt

Serves 4 • Preparation 15 minutes + 30 minutes to cool + time to churn
Cooking: 2–3 minutes • Difficulty 1

1. Combine the sugar and water in a medium saucepan over medium heat and bring to a boil. Simmer, stirring often, until the sugar has dissolved, 2–3 minutes. Set aside to cool for 30 minutes.

2. Chop the strawberries in a food processor until smooth. Stir into the cooled sugar syrup. Stir in the yogurt until smooth.

3. Transfer to your ice cream machine and churn according to the manufacturer's instructions.

4. Spoon or pipe the sorbet into serving bowls or glasses.

If you liked this recipe, you will love these as well.

STRAWBERRY spumone

WHITE CHOCOLATE
& STRAWBERRY parfait

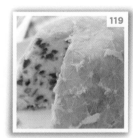
RICOTTA
& STRAWBERRY dome

GRAPE sorbet

1½   pounds (750 g) white grapes,
     preferably seedless
½   cup (100 g) superfine (caster)
     sugar
⅓   cup (90 ml) dry white wine
2   tablespoons grappa
     (or brandy)

Serves 4–6 • Preparation 15 minutes + time to churn • Difficulty 1

1. Rinse the grapes well and—if you are not using a seedless variety—remove the seeds. Reserve a few grapes to decorate. Chop the remaining grapes in a food processor. Strain through a fine-mesh sieve to remove the skins.

2. Measure out 1½ cups (375 ml) of grape juice and pour into a bowl. Add the sugar, wine, and grappa and stir until the sugar is completely dissolved.

3. Transfer to your ice cream machine and churn according to the manufacturer's instructions.

4. Spoon or pipe the sorbet into serving bowls or glasses and decorate with the reserved grapes.

RASPBERRY sorbet

³/₄ cup (150 g) sugar
¹/₂ cup (125 ml) water
2 pounds (1 kg) raspberries
¹/₄ cup (60 ml) freshly squeezed
lemon juice

Serves 4 • Preparation 20 minutes + 30 minutes to chill + time to churn
Cooking 2–3 minutes • Difficulty 1

1. Combine the sugar and water in a small saucepan over medium heat and bring to a boil. Simmer, stirring often, until the sugar has dissolved, 2–3 minutes. Set aside.

2. Put the raspberries and lemon juice in a food processor and blend until puréed. Pass through a fine-mesh sieve to remove the seeds. Add the sugar syrup and stir to combine. Chill in the refrigerator for 30 minutes.

3. Transfer to your ice cream machine and churn according to the manufacturer's instructions.

4. Spoon or pipe the sorbet into serving bowls or glasses.

Prepare this sorbet at the height of summer when peaches are at their fragrant best. For apricot sorbet, replace the peaches in this recipe with the same weight of ripe apricots.

PEACH sorbet

1³/₄ cups (350 g) sugar

1¹/₂ cups (375 ml) water

1¹/₂ pounds (750 g) very ripe white peaches, peeled, pitted, and thinly sliced

Freshly squeezed juice of 2 lemons

1 large egg white

Serves 4 • Preparation 15 minutes + 30 minutes to cool + time to churn
Cooking 2-3 minutes • Difficulty 1

1. Combine the sugar and water in a saucepan over medium heat and bring to a boil. Simmer, stirring often, until the sugar has dissolved, 2–3 minutes. Set aside to cool for 30 minutes.

2. Press the peaches through a fine-mesh sieve or chop in a food processor until smooth. You should have just over 1 pound (500 g) of peach purée. Stir the peach purée and lemon juice into the cooled sugar syrup.

3. Beat the egg white with an electric mixer on high speed until stiff. Fold into the peach mixture.

4. Transfer to your ice cream machine and churn according to the manufacturer's instructions.

5. Spoon or pipe the sorbet into serving bowls or glasses.

If you liked this recipe, you will love these as well.

CHERRY BRANDY
sorbet

GRAPE sorbet

LEMON SORBET
with strawberries

You can vary this recipe by using red or white currants instead of the black ones. The red currants make a striking, bright red sorbet.

BLACKCURRANT sorbet

- $3/4$ cup (150 g) sugar
- $2/3$ cup (180 ml) water
- 1 pound (500 g) fresh ripe black currants
- Freshly squeezed juice of $1/2$ lemon
- 1 small egg white
- Whipped cream, to serve (optional)

Serves 4-6 • Preparation 20 minutes + 30 minutes to cool + time to churn • Cooking 2-3 minutes • Difficulty 1

1. Combine the sugar and water in a saucepan over medium heat. Bring to a boil and simmer, stirring often, until the sugar has dissolved, 2-3 minutes. Set aside to cool for 30 minutes.

2. Rinse the black currants in ice cold water and drain well. Place the black currants and lemon juice in a food processor and chop until smooth. Press the purée through a fine mesh sieve, collecting the strained purée in a bowl.

3. Stir the black currant purée into the cooled syrup. Transfer the mixture to your ice cream machine and churn according to the manufacturer's instructions.

4. Beat the egg white in a small bowl with an electric mixer on high speed until stiff. When the ice cream machine is half way through its cycle, fold in the egg white, then let the machine complete its cycle.

5. Spoon or pipe the sorbet into serving bowls or glasses.

If you liked this recipe, you will love these as well.

AMARENA CHERRY
ice cream
38

BLACKBERRY
sorbet
66

RED CURRANT
granita
76

SAGE sorbet

Serves 4 • Preparation 10 minutes 1½ hours to infuse
& freeze + time to churn • Cooking 2–3 minutes • Difficulty 2

³/₄	cup (150 g) sugar	10	fresh sage leaves +
1¹/₃	cups (350 ml) water		extra leaves to garnish
1	ounce (30 g) glucose		
	or 2 tablespoons light		
	corn (golden) syrup		

1. Place the sugar and 1 cup (250 ml) of water in a saucepan over medium heat and bring to a boil. Simmer, stirring often, until the sugar has dissolved, 2–3 minutes. Remove from the heat and add the glucose and sage leaves. Set aside to infuse for 30 minutes.

2. Discard the sage leaves and add the remaining ¹/₃ cup (90 ml) water. Freeze for 1 hour.

3. Transfer to an ice cream machine and churn according to the manufacturer's instructions.

4. Spoon or pipe the sorbet into serving glasses or bowls and garnish with fresh sage leaves.

BASIL sorbet

Serves 4 • Preparation 10 minutes + 1½ hours to infuse
& freeze + time to churn • Cooking 2–3 minutes • Difficulty 2

³/₄	cup (150 g) sugar	15	leaves fresh basil +
1¹/₃	cups (350 ml) water		extra leaves to garnish
1	ounce (30 g) glucose	2–3	drops green food
	or 2 tablespoons light		coloring
	corn (golden) syrup		Balsamic vinegar

1. Combine the sugar and 1 cup (250 ml) of water in a saucepan over medium heat and bring to a boil. Simmer, stirring often, until the sugar has dissolved, 2–3 minutes. Remove from the heat and add the glucose and 15 basil leaves. Set aside to infuse for 30 minutes.

2. Discard the basil leaves and add the remaining ¹/₃ cup (90 ml) of water. Stir in the food coloring and freeze for 1 hour.

3. Transfer to an ice cream machine and churn according to the manufacturer's instructions. Add a splash or two of balsamic vinegar to the machine about 30 seconds before the sorbet is ready.

4. Spoon or pipe the sorbet into serving glasses or bowls and garnish with fresh basil leaves.

CELERY & STAR ANISE sorbet

Serves 4 • Preparation 10 minutes + 1½ hours to infuse
& freeze + time to churn • Cooking 2–3 minutes • Difficulty 2

1	cup (200 g) sugar	4	large tender celery
1¹/₃	cups (330 ml) water		stalks, leaves removed
1	star anise		and chopped

1. Combine the sugar, ³/₄ cup (200 ml) of water, and star anise in a saucepan over medium heat and bring to a boil. Simmer, stirring often, until the sugar has dissolved, 2–3 minutes. Set aside to infuse for 30 minutes. Discard the star anise.

2. Chop the celery with ¹/₄ cup (60 ml) of water in a food processor until smooth. Strain through a fine-mesh sieve to eliminate any tough fibers.

3. Stir into the cooled sugar syrup, adding the remaining ¹/₃ cup (90 ml) of cold water. Freeze for 1 hour.

4. Transfer to your ice cream machine and churn according to the manufacturer's instructions.

5. Spoon or pipe the sorbet into serving glasses or bowls.

TOMATO sorbet

Serves 4 • Preparation 20 minutes + 1½ hours to cool
& freeze + time to churn • Cooking 3–4 minutes • Difficulty 2

14	ounces (400 g) ripe	²/₃	cup (180 ml) water
	tomatoes, peeled	¹/₄	teaspoon salt
³/₄	cup (150 g) sugar		

1. Chop the tomatoes into small cubes. Place in a saucepan over medium heat and simmer until they release their water, 3–4 minutes. Remove from the heat and process in a food mill or food processor. Strain through a fine-mesh sieve and weigh out 8 ounces (250 g) of purée.

2. Combine the sugar and ¹/₃ cup (90 ml) of water in a saucepan over medium heat. Bring to a boil and simmer, stirring often, until the sugar has dissolved, 2–3 minutes. Set aside to cool for 30 minutes.

3. Stir in the tomato purée, the remaining ¹/₃ cup (90 ml) water, and the salt and let cool completely. Chill in the freezer for 1 hour.

4. Transfer to your ice cream machine and churn according to the manufacturer's instructions.

LEMON SORBET with strawberries

1   cup (200 g) sugar
1¼   cups (300 ml) water
       Freshly squeezed juice
       of 4 lemons
3   large egg whites
⅛   teaspoon salt
       Sliced strawberries, to serve

Serves 4 • Preparation 20 minutes + 30 minutes to cool + time to churn • Cooking 2–3 minutes • Difficulty 1

1. Combine the sugar and water in a small saucepan over medium heat and bring to a boil. Simmer, stirring often, until the sugar has dissolved, 2–3 minutes. Set aside to cool for 30 minutes.

2. Stir the lemon juice into the sugar syrup. Transfer the mixture to your ice cream machine and churn according to the manufacturer's instructions.

3. Beat the egg whites and salt in a small bowl with an electric mixer on high speed until stiff. When the ice cream machine is half way through its cycle, fold in the egg white, then let the machine complete its cycle.

4. Spoon or pipe the sorbet into serving bowls or glasses and garnish with the strawberries.

CHOCOLATE MINT sorbet

2¾ cups (680 ml) water
1 cup (200 g) sugar
1 cup (150 g) unsweetened cocoa powder
4 sprigs fresh mint, finely chopped
Ice cream wafers or other thin, crisp cookies, to serve

Serves 4–6 • Preparation 20 minutes + 30 minutes to cool + time to churn • Cooking 12–13 minutes • Difficulty 1

1. Combine the water and sugar in a medium saucepan over medium heat and bring to a boil. Simmer, stirring often, until the sugar has dissolved, 2–3 minutes. Stir in the cocoa powder and mint. Simmer over very low heat for 10 minutes. Set aside to cool for 30 minutes.

2. Transfer the mixture to your ice cream machine and churn according to the manufacturer's instructions.

3. Spoon or pipe the sorbet into serving bowls or glasses.

This recipe makes a rich dark-red sorbet which is only slightly tempered by the cream. You can vary the recipe by using the same quantity of boysenberries or raspberries, or a mixture of the two.

BLACKBERRY sorbet

1	pound (500 g) fresh ripe blackberries
1	cup (200 g) sugar
1	cup (250 ml) water
	Freshly squeezed juice of 1 lemon
$1/4$	cup (60 ml) heavy (double) cream

Serves 4 • Preparation 20 minutes + 30 minutes to rest + time to churn • Cooking 2-3 minutes • Difficulty 1

1. Rinse the blackberries under cold running water and place in a bowl without draining well. Sprinkle with 2 tablespoons of sugar and drizzle with the lemon juice. Set aside for 30 minutes.

2. Combine the remaining sugar and water in a saucepan over medium heat. Bring to a boil and simmer, stirring often, until the sugar has dissolved, 2–3 minutes. Set aside to cool.

3. Pass the blackberries through a food mill or chop in a food processor. Strain through a fine-mesh sieve to remove the seeds. Stir the purée into the cooled sugar syrup.

4. Beat the cream in a small bowl with an electric mixer on high speed until thick. Fold into the blackberry mixture. Transfer to your ice cream machine and freeze following the manufacturer's instructions.

5. Spoon or pipe the sorbet into serving bowls or glasses.

If you liked this recipe, you will love these as well.

STRAWBERRY YOGURT
sorbet

BLACKCURRANT
sorbet

BLACKBERRY
granita

NUTTY spumone

3   cups (750 ml) milk
1   cup (200 g) sugar
5   large eggs, separated
1/2   teaspoon salt
1 1/2   cups (375 ml) heavy (double)
         cream
1/2   cup (70 g) finely ground
         almonds
1/2   cup (70 g) finely ground
         hazelnuts
1   teaspoon vanilla extract
         (essence)
1/2   teaspoon almond extract
         (essence)

Serves 4–6 • Preparation 30 minutes + 30 minutes to cool + time to churn • Cooking: 10–15 minutes • Difficulty 2

1. Combine the milk, sugar, egg yolks, and salt in a double boiler over barely simmering water. Stir until the mixture thickens, 10–15 minutes. Set aside for 30 minutes to cool.

2. Beat the egg whites in a bowl with an electric mixer on high speed until stiff. Beat the cream in a large bowl with mixer on high speed until thick. Fold the egg whites, cream, almonds, hazelnuts, vanilla extract, and almond extract into the milk mixture.

3. Transfer to your ice cream machine and churn according to the manufacturer's instructions until creamy but not quite frozen.

4. Spoon or pipe the spumone into serving bowls or glasses.

STRAWBERRY spumone

1   pound (500 g) strawberries, sliced
1½   cups (300 g) sugar
1   cup (250 ml) heavy (double) cream
⅛   teaspoon salt

Serves 4 • Preparation 20 minutes + 2 hours to rest + time to churn
Difficulty 2

1. Put the strawberries in a large bowl and sprinkle with the sugar. Cover and let rest for 2 hours.

2. Place the cream in the freezer until it begins to thicken, about 1 hour.

3. Transfer the strawberries and their juices to a food processor and blend until smooth. Strain into a large bowl through a fine-mesh sieve.

4. Gradually stir the cream and salt into the strawberry mixture. Transfer the mixture to your ice cream machine and churn according to the manufacturer's instructions until creamy but not quite frozen.

5. Spoon or pipe the spumone into the chilled glasses.

granitas

PEACH granita

2 pounds (1 kg) ripe peaches, peeled, pitted, and cut into small cubes + 1 extra small peach, pitted and cut into small cubes to garnish

1⅓ cups (350 ml) water

½ cup (100 g) sugar

Chilled peach vodka to serve (optional)

Serves 4-6 • Preparation 15 minutes + 30 minutes to cool + time to freeze • Cooking 10 minutes • Difficulty 2

1. Combine the peaches and 1 cup (250 ml) of water in a medium saucepan over medium heat. Cover and simmer, stirring occasionally, until the peaches are softened, about 10 minutes.

2. Remove from the heat, add the sugar, and stir until the sugar is dissolved. Let cool to room temperature.

3. Purée the cooled peach mixture in a blender with the remaining ⅓ cup (90 ml) of water until smooth.

4. Pour the mixture into a large shallow freezerproof container. Cover with plastic wrap (cling film). Freeze until almost solid, 1-2 hours. Use a fork or hand-held beater to break the granita up into large crystals. Replace the container in the freezer until almost frozen again, about 1 hour, then break it up again with a fork. Repeat three or four times, until the crystals are separate and completely frozen.

5. Serve the granita in serving glasses or bowls garnished with the peac and drizzled with the vodka, if desired.

If you liked this recipe, you will love these as well.

PEACH sorbet

FROZEN BELLINI granita

MELON granita

Granita is a flavored ice with a grainy texture that falls somewhere between a slushy and a sorbet. It originally comes from Sicily, where it is has been made for centuries. Traditional Sicilian flavors include coffee, lemon, almond, mandarin, orange, and mint. Coffee or almond granitas are often served at breakfast, along with a Sicilian brioche.

COFFEE granita

1 cup (200 g) sugar
1½ tablespoons unsweetened cocoa powder
½ cup (125 ml) water
5 cups (1.25 liters) very strong brewed black coffee

Serves 6-8 • Preparation 15 minutes + 30 minutes to cool + time to freeze • Cooking 5 minutes • Difficulty 2

1. Combine the sugar and cocoa in a large saucepan over medium-low heat. Slowly mix in the water until smooth. Bring to a boil, stirring often, until the sugar has dissolved. Decrease the heat to low and simmer for 3 minutes.

2. Remove from the heat and stir in the coffee. Pour the mixture into a shallow freezerproof container and let cool to room temperature, about 30 minutes. Cover with plastic wrap (cling film).

3. Freeze until almost solid, 1–2 hours. Use a fork or hand-held beater to break the granita up into large crystals. Replace the container in the freezer until almost frozen again, about 1 hour, then break up again with a fork. Repeat three or four times, until the crystals are separate and completely frozen.

4. Serve in espresso cups.

If you liked this recipe, you will love these as well.

COFFEE GRANITA
with chocolate & cream

CARAMEL LATTE
granita

MOCHA semifreddo

COFFEE GRANITA with chocolate & cream

2   cups (500 ml) water

³/₄   cup (150 g) superfine (caster) sugar

4   tablespoons instant coffee granules

2   tablespoons unsweetened cocoa powder

1   cup (250 ml) whipped cream

3   tablespoons finely grated dark chocolate to garnish

Serves 4 • Preparation 20 minutes + 30 minutes to cool + time to freeze
Cooking 1 minute • Difficulty 2

1. Combine 1¹/₂ cups (375 ml) of water with the sugar in a saucepan over medium heat and bring to a boil. Simmer for 1 minute. Set aside to cool, about 30 minutes.

2. Put the remaining water in a medium bowl and mix in the coffee and cocoa until smooth. Stir in the sugar syrup. Pour into a shallow freezerproof container. Cover with plastic wrap (cling film).

3. Freeze until almost solid, 1–2 hours. Use a fork or hand-held beater to break up into large crystals. Replace in the freezer until almost frozen again, about 1 hour, then break it up again with a fork. Repeat three or four times, until the crystals are separate and completely frozen.

4. Spoon the granita into glasses. Top with cream and chocolate.

CARAMEL LATTE granita

1½ cups (375 ml) cold expresso coffee

1 cup (250 ml) milk

5 tablespoons (75 ml) caramel syrup

½ cup (125 ml) whipped cream

2 tablespoons finely grated dark chocolate to garnish

1. Combine the coffee, milk, and caramel syrup in a bowl. Stir until well mixed. Pour the mixture into a shallow freezerproof container. Cover with plastic wrap (cling film).

2. Freeze until almost solid, 1–2 hours. Use a fork or hand-held beater to break up into large crystals. Replace in the freezer until almost frozen again, about 1 hour, then break it up again with a fork. Repeat three or four times, until the crystals are separate and completely frozen.

3. Spoon into expresso cups or small glasses and top with small dollop of cream. Sprinkle with the chocolate.

RED CURRANT granita

Serves 6–8 • Preparation 10 minutes + 30 minutes to cool + time to freeze • Difficulty 2

1½	pounds (750 g) fresh red currants + extra to garnish	¾	cup (150 g) sugar
		1¼	cups (300 ml) water

1. Put the red currants in a large bowl and mash with a fork. Press through a fine-mesh sieve to eliminate the seeds.

2. Combine the sugar and water in a saucepan over medium heat and stir until the sugar is dissolved. Let cool to room temperature, about 30 minutes.

3. Stir the red currant purée into the sugar syrup. Pour the mixture into a shallow freezerproof container. Cover with plastic wrap (cling film).

4. Freeze until almost solid, 1–2 hours. Use a fork or hand-held beater to break up into large crystals. Replace in the freezer until almost frozen again, about 1 hour, then break it up again with a fork. Repeat three or four times, until the crystals are separate and completely frozen.

5. Spoon into glasses and garnish with extra bunches of red (or black or white) currants.

LEMON granita

Serves 4–6 • Preparation 10 minutes + 30 minutes to cool + time to freeze • Difficulty 2

1½	cups (375 ml) water	Sliced fresh strawberries to garnish (optional)
¾	cup (150 g) sugar	
1	cup (250 ml) freshly squeezed lemon juice	

1. Combine the water and sugar in a medium saucepan over low heat and stir until the sugar is dissolved. Remove from the heat and let cool to room temperature, about 30 minutes.

2. Stir in the lemon juice then pour the syrup into a shallow freezerproof container. Cover with plastic wrap (cling film).

3. Freeze until almost solid, 1–2 hours. Use a fork or hand-held beater to break up into large crystals. Replace in the freezer until almost frozen again, about 1 hour, then break it up again with a fork. Repeat three or four times, until the crystals are separate and completely frozen.

4. Spoon the granita into small glasses and garnish with sliced strawberries, if liked.

PROSECCO granita

Serves 4–6 • Preparation 10 minutes + 1 hour to rest + time to freeze • Difficulty 2

1	cup (250 ml) water		orange
½	cup (100 g) sugar	1	cinnamon stick, broken
	Freshly squeezed juice of 3 lemons + 1 whole lemon	4	cloves
		1	bottle (750 ml) Prosecco (or Champagne)
	Freshly squeezed juice of 2 oranges + 1 whole		Candied (glacé) cherries to garnish

1. Combine the water, sugar, lemon juice, orange juice, cinnamon, and cloves in a medium bowl. Peel the whole orange and lemon. Cut into segments and add to the bowl. Mix well and let rest for 1 hour.

2. Filter through a fine-mesh sieve. Stir the Prosecco into the filtered liquid. Pour into a shallow freezer-proof container. Cover with plastic wrap (cling film).

3. Freeze until almost solid, 1–2 hours. Use a fork or hand-held beater to break up into large crystals. Replace in the freezer until almost frozen again, about 1 hour, then break it up again with a fork. Repeat three or four times, until the crystals are separate and completely frozen.

4. Spoon into champagne flutes or wine goblets and garnish with the cherries.

FROZEN BELLINI granita

Serves 6 • Preparation 10 minutes + 30 minutes to cool + time to freeze • Difficulty 2

½	cup (125 ml) water	6	juicy white peaches, peeled, pitted, and coarsely hopped
¾	cup (150 g) sugar		
	Finely grated zest of ½ organic lemon	2	cups (500 ml) Prosecco or very dry Champagne
	Freshly squeezed juice of 1 lemon		

1. Combine the water, sugar, and lemon zest and juice in a small saucepan over low heat and stir until the sugar has completely dissolved. Let cool to room temperature, about 30 minutes.

2. Put the peaches in a blender with the cooled sugar syrup and chop until smooth. Stir in the Prosecco. Pour into a shallow freezerproof container. Cover with plastic wrap (cling film).

3. Freeze until almost solid, 1–2 hours. Use a fork or hand-held beater to break up into large crystals. Replace in the freezer until almost frozen again, about 1 hour, then break it up again with a fork. Repeat three or four times, until the crystals are separate and completely frozen.

4. Spoon into champagne flutes or wine goblets.

Choose fragrant cantaloupe (rock) melons at the height of summer for best results with this strikingly pretty granita.

MELON granita

4   cups (600 g) chopped
     cantaloupe (rock) melon
1¹/₂ cups (350 ml) dry
     Champagne
³/₄   cup (150 g) sugar
2   tablespoons freshly squeezed
     lemon juice

Serves 4-6 • Preparation 20 minutes + time to freeze • Difficulty 2

1. Purée the melon in a food processor. Transfer to a large bowl and add the Champagne, sugar, and lemon juice. Stir gently until the sugar is dissolved.

2. Pour into a shallow freezerproof container. Cover with plastic wrap (cling film). Freeze until almost solid, 1–2 hours. Use a fork or hand-held beater to break up into large crystals. Replace in the freezer until almost frozen again, about 1 hour, then break it up again with a fork. Repeat three or four times, until the crystals are separate and completely frozen.

3. Spoon into wine glasses or champagne flutes.

If you liked this recipe, you will love these as well.

MELON sorbet

PEACH granita

GRAPEFRUIT
& CAMPARI granita

STRAWBERRY GRANITA with cream

2   cups (500 ml) water
³/₄   cup (150 g) sugar
1   pound (500 g) fresh
         strawberries
¹/₃   cup (90 ml) heavy (double)
         cream
1   tablespoon confectioners'
         (icing) sugar

Serves 4–6 • Preparation 20 minutes + 30 minutes to cool + time to freeze • Cooking 2–3 minutes • Difficulty 2

1. Combine the water and sugar in a medium saucepan. Bring to a boil over medium heat, stirring often, until the sugar has dissolved, 2–3 minutes. Let cool, about 30 minutes.

2. Purée the strawberries in a food processor. Stir the purée into the cooled syrup.

3. Pour into a shallow freezerproof container. Cover with plastic wrap (cling film). Freeze until almost solid, 1–2 hours. Use a fork or hand-held beater to break up into large crystals. Replace in the freezer until almost frozen again, about 1 hour, then break it up again with a fork. Repeat three or four times, until the crystals are separate and completely frozen.

4. Beat the cream and confectioners' sugar until thickened. Spoon the granita into dessert glasses and top with cream.

ORANGE granita

2 cups (500 ml) freshly squeezed orange juice

¾ cup (200 ml) dry white wine

¼ cup (60 ml) Grand Marnier or other orange-flavored liqueur

¼ cup (50 g) sugar

1 tablespoon finely grated organic orange zest

Shredded mint, to garnish

Serves 4 • Preparation 20 minutes • Cooking 2-3 minutes • Difficulty 2

1. Combine the orange juice, wine, Grand Marnier, sugar, and orange zest in a medium saucepan. Bring to a boil over medium-low heat, stirring often, until the sugar has dissolved, 2-3 minutes. Let cool to room temperature, about 30 minutes.

2. Pour into a shallow freezerproof container. Cover with plastic wrap (cling film). Freeze until almost solid, 1-2 hours. Use a fork or hand-held beater to break up into large crystals. Replace in the freezer until almost frozen again, about 1 hour, then break it up again with a fork. Repeat three or four times, until the crystals are separate and completely frozen.

3. Spoon into glasses and serve.

Rasberries make a striking, bright red granita. Decorate with a little whipped cream if liked. If serving this dessert to children, use a raspberry-flavored syrup instead of the raspberry liqueur.

RASPBERRY granita

3	cups (750 ml) water
1	cup (200 g) sugar
4	cups (600 g) fresh raspberries + a few extra to garnish
1	tablespoon freshly squeezed lemon juice
1/3	cup (90 ml) Chambord (raspberry liqueur)

Serves 4–6 • Preparation 15 minutes + 30 minutes to cool + time to freeze • Cooking 2–3 minutes • Difficulty 2

1. Combine 1 cup (250 ml) of water with the sugar in a saucepan. Bring to a boil over medium-low heat, stirring often, until the sugar has dissolved, 2–3 minutes. Let cool to room temperature, about 30 minutes.

2. Purée the raspberries in a food processor or mash with a fork until smooth. Press the mixture through a fine-mesh sieve to remove the seeds.

3. Stir the lemon juice, remaining 2 cups (500 ml) of water, and the Chambord into the raspberry mixture. Stir in the sugar syrup and mix well.

4. Pour into a shallow freezerproof container. Cover with plastic wrap (cling film). Freeze until almost solid, 1–2 hours. Use a fork or hand-held beater to break up into large crystals. Replace in the freezer until almost frozen again, about 1 hour, then break it up again with a fork. Repeat three or four times, until the crystals are separate and completely frozen.

If you liked this recipe, you will love these as well.

RASPBERRY sorbet

EASY RASPBERRY granita

BLACKBERRY granita

GRAPEFRUIT & CAMPARI granita

1 cup (250 ml) freshly squeezed
   pink grapefruit juice, strained
1 cup (250 ml) water
1 cup (200 g) sugar
1 sprig fresh mint
3 tablespoons Campari
2 tablespoons freshly squeezed
   lemon juice

Serves 4 • Preparation 15 minutes + 30 minutes to chill + time to freeze
Cooking 2–3 minutes • Difficulty 2

1. Combine the grapefruit juice, water, sugar, and mint in a small saucepan over medium heat. Bring to a boil, stirring often, until the sugar has dissolved, 2–3 minutes.

2. Pour the mixture into a medium bowl. Discard the mint. Stir in the Campari and lemon juice and refrigerate until cooled, about 30 minutes.

3. Pour the mixture into a shallow freezerproof container. Cover with plastic wrap (cling film). Freeze until almost solid, 1–2 hours. Use a fork or hand-held beater to break up into large crystals. Replace in the freezer until almost frozen again, about 1 hour, then break it up again with a fork. Repeat three or four times, until the crystals are separate and completely frozen.

RED WINE granita

3/4 cup (150 g) sugar
Finely grated zest of 1 orange
Freshly squeezed juice of 1 orange
Freshly squeezed of 1 lemon
1 cinnamon stick
2 cloves
1/2 cup (125 ml) water
1 bottle (750 ml) red wine

Serves 4–6 • Preparation 20 minutes + 30 minutes to cool + time to freeze • Cooking 2–3 minutes • Difficulty 2

1. Combine all the ingredients in a saucepan. Bring to a boil over medium-low heat, stirring often, until the sugar has dissolved, 2–3 minutes. Let cool to room temperature, about 30 minutes.

2. Strain the mixture through a fine-mesh sieve. Pour the mixture into a shallow freezerproof container. Cover with plastic wrap (cling film).

3. Freeze until almost solid, 1–2 hours. Use a fork or hand-held beater to break up into large crystals. Replace in the freezer until almost frozen again, about 1 hour, then break it up again with a fork. Repeat three or four times, until the crystals are separate and completely frozen.

A mojito is a traditional Cuban cocktail made with five ingredients: white rum, sugar, lime, mint, and water. Our mojito granita replicates these flavors in a refreshing iced drink that makes a delicious appetizer or pre-dinner drink on hot summer nights.

MOJITO granita

2¹/₂ cups (600 ml) water
¹/₂   cup (100 g) sugar
      Finely grated zest of 2 limes
1   cup (50 g) fresh mint leaves + 8 extra leaves, finely chopped
¹/₂   cup (125 ml) freshly squeezed lime juice
3   tablespoons white rum + extra to serve

Serves 4-6 • Preparation 15 minutes + 30 minutes to cool + time to freeze • Cooking 5 minutes • Difficulty 2

1. Combine the water, sugar, and lime zest in a small saucepan. Bring to a boil over medium-low heat, stirring constantly until the sugar has dissolved, 2–3 minutes. Add the mint leaves and remove from the heat. Cover and let sit for 10 minutes. Uncover the saucepan and let cool to room temperature, about 30 minutes.

2. Strain the mixture into a shallow freezerproof container, pressing on the leaves to extract all the flavor. Discard the whole mint leaves. Stir in the lime juice, rum, and finely chopped mint leaves. Cover with plastic wrap (cling film).

3. Freeze until almost solid, 1–2 hours. Use a fork or hand-held beater to break up into large crystals. Replace in the freezer until almost frozen again, about 1 hour, then break it up again with a fork. Repeat three or four times, until the crystals are separate and completely frozen.

4. Spoon into glasses and drizzle a bit of extra rum over each serving, if desired.

If you liked this recipe, you will love these as well.

PROSECCO granita

FROZEN BELLINI granita

GRAPEFRUIT & CAMPARI granita

CITRUS TEA granita

2 cups (500 ml) water

1 teaspoon loose tea leaves

Generous 1/2 cup (125 g) sugar

Finely grated zest and freshly squeezed juice of 1 organic orange

Finely grated zest and freshly squeezed juice of 1 organic lime + peel to garnish

1/4 cup (60 ml) dark rum

1/2 teaspoon vanilla extract (essence)

Serves 4–6 • Preparation 20 minutes + 30 minutes to cool + time to freeze • Cooking 2–3 minutes • Difficulty 2

1. Bring 1 cup (250 ml) of the water to a boil. Put the tea into a teapot and cover with the water. Let brew for 10 minutes. Strain and let cool completely.

2. Put the remaining 1 cup (250 ml) of water in a small saucepan with the sugar and orange and lime zests. Bring to a boil over medium heat, stirring often, until the sugar has dissolved, 2–3 minutes. Let cool to room temperature, about 30 minutes.

3. Stir in the rum, tea, orange juice, lime juice, and vanilla. Pour the mixture into a shallow freezerproof container. Cover with plastic wrap (cling film).

4. Freeze until almost solid, 1–2 hours. Use a fork or hand-held beater to break up into large crystals. Replace in the freezer until almost frozen again, about 1 hour, then break it up again with a fork. Repeat three or four times, until the crystals are separate and completely frozen.

5. Spoon into glasses and garnish with the lime peel.

ORANGE & GINGER granita

3   cups (750 ml) freshly
    squeezed orange juice
1   tablespoon finely grated
    organic orange zest
2   teaspoons finely grated fresh
    ginger
3/4 cup (150 g) sugar
    Fresh mint leaves to garnish

Serves 4–6 • Preparation 20 minutes + 30 minutes to chill + time to freeze • Cooking 2–3 minutes • Difficulty 2

1. Combine the orange juice, zest ginger, and sugar in a medium saucepan. Bring to a boil over medium-low heat, stirring often, until the sugar has dissolved, 2–3 minutes. Let cool to room temperature, about 30 minutes.

2. Pour the mixture into a shallow freezerproof container. Cover with plastic wrap (cling film). Freeze until almost solid, 1–2 hours. Use a fork or hand-held beater to break up into large crystals. Replace in the freezer until almost frozen again, about 1 hour, then break it up again with a fork. Repeat three or four times, until the crystals are separate and completely frozen.

3. Spoon into serving glasses and garnish with the mint.

EASY RASPBERRY granita

1   pound (500 g) fresh
     raspberries + a few extra
     to garnish
2   tablespoons sugar
     Freshly squeezed juice
     of 1 lime
2   cups (500 ml) crushed ice

Serves 4 • Preparation 15 minutes + 2 hours to macerate + time to freeze • Difficulty 1

1. Put the raspberries in a medium bowl. Sprinkle with the sugar and drizzle with the lime juice. Cover with plastic wrap (cling film) and let macerate for 2 hours.

2. Mash the raspberry mixture with a fork until smooth. Press through a fine-mesh sieve to eliminate the seeds.

3. Divide the crushed ice evenly among chilled serving glasses. Pour an equal amount of the raspberry purée over the ice into each glass. Garnish with fresh raspberries.

BLACKBERRY granita

1½ pounds (750 g) fresh ripe blackberries
¾ cup (150 g) sugar
1¼ cups (300 ml) water

Serves 4–6 • Preparation 20 minutes + 30 minutes to cool + time to freeze • Cooking: 2–3 minutes • Difficulty 2

1. Put the blackberries in a large bowl and mash with a fork. Press through a fine-mesh sieve to eliminate the seeds.

2. Combine the sugar and water in a saucepan over medium-low heat and stir until the sugar is dissolved, 2–3 minutes. Let cool to room temperature, about 30 minutes.

3. Stir the blackberry purée into the sugar syrup. Pour the mixture into a shallow freezerproof container. Cover with plastic wrap (cling film).

4. Freeze until almost solid, 1–2 hours. Use a fork or hand-held beater to break up into large crystals. Replace in the freezer until almost frozen again, about 1 hour, then break it up again with a fork. Repeat three or four times, until the crystals are separate and completely frozen.

cool desserts

CHOCOLATE MASCARPONE semifreddo

4   ounces (125 g) dark chocolate, chopped
3   tablespoons milk
2   large egg yolks
$1/2$ cup (100 g) sugar
$1^1/_3$ cups (300 g) mascarpone cheese
1   tablespoon Marsala wine
6   ready-made plain meringues
    Grated dark chocolate, to decorate

Serves 4–6 • Preparation 15 minutes + 2 hours to chill • Cooking 5 minutes • Difficulty 1

1. Stir the chocolate and milk in a double boiler over barely simmering water until melted and smooth. Set aside to cool.

2. Beat the egg yolks and sugar in a medium bowl with an electric mixer on high speed until pale and creamy.

3. Carefully stir in the mascarpone and Marsala. Divide the mixture equally between two bowls.

4. Stir the chocolate mixture into one bowl.

5. Crumble the meringues into the bottoms of 4–6 glasses or serving bowls and add alternate spoonfuls of the plain mascarpone and chocolate mascarpone mixtures. Top with grated chocolate.

6. Chill in the refrigerator for at least 2 hours before serving.

If you liked this recipe, you will love these as well.

MILK CHOCOLATE
semifreddo

CHOCOLATE
semifreddo

ZABAGLIONE
semifreddo

A semifreddo (meaning "half frozen") is an Italian dessert usually based on a flavored cream or custard which is chilled without being fully frozen. Crumbled meringue is often added to stop the dessert from freezing solid.

MILK CHOCOLATE semifreddo

4 ounces (120 g) milk chocolate, chopped + extra to decorate
$2^1/_3$ cups (600 ml) heavy (double) cream
2 large eggs, separated
$2/_3$ cup (130 g) superfine (caster) sugar
1 teaspoon vanilla extract (essence)

Serves 4 • Preparation 20 minutes + 12 hours to freeze • Cooking 5 minutes • Difficulty 1

1. Place the chocolate in a bowl. Bring $3/_4$ cup (200 ml) of the cream to a boil over medium heat and pour over the chocolate. Stir until melted and smooth. Let cool.

2. Beat the egg yolks and half the sugar with an electric mixer on high speed until pale and creamy.

3. Beat the egg whites and remaining sugar until stiff peaks form. Fold the whites into the egg yolk mixture. Whip the remaining cream until thick. Fold into the egg mixture.

4. Divide the mixture between two bowls, placing one-third in one, and two-thirds in the other. Stir the vanilla into the smaller mixture. Fold the chocolate into larger mixture.

5. Pour the vanilla mixture into four 1-cup (250-ml) ramekins. Freeze until firm, about 30 minutes. Spoon in the chocolate mixture and freeze overnight.

6. To serve, dip the base of each ramekin into hot water and shake out. Place on a tray and freeze for a few minutes before transferring to serving plates. Sprinkle with chocolate.

If you liked this recipe, you will love these as well.

CHOCOLATE MASCARPONE semifreddo

MOCHA semifreddo

CHOCOLATE SEMIFREDDO with cherry compote

CHOCOLATE semifreddo

Serves 4–6 • Preparation 20 minutes + 6 hours to freeze
Cooking 10 minutes • Difficulty 2

4	ounces (125 g) dark chocolate, chopped + extra to serve	1	teaspoon vanilla extract (essence)
1	cup (250 ml) milk	2	large egg whites
1/3	cup (75 g) sugar	2/3	cup (100 g) confectioners' (icing) sugar
2	large egg yolks	1	teaspoon lemon juice
1/3	cup (30 g) all-purpose (plain) flour	2	cups (500 ml) heavy (double) cream

1. Stir the chocolate in a double boiler over barely simmering water until melted. Set aside.

2. Bring the milk to a boil over low heat. Beat the egg yolks, sugar, flour, and vanilla until pale and creamy. Pour the hot milk into the egg mixture, beating constantly. Return to the saucepan over low heat, beating constantly, until thick, 4–5 minutes. Let cool.

3. Beat the egg whites, confectioners' sugar, and lemon juice in a double boiler over barely simmering water until thick and creamy. Remove from the heat. Beat the cream until thick. Fold the egg white mixture into the egg cream, then fold in the cream and chocolate.

4. Spoon into 4–6 ramekins and freeze for 6 hours. Decorate with the extra chocolate and cream.

MOCHA semifreddo

Serves 4–6 • Preparation 20 minutes + 4 hours to freeze
Cooking 10 minutes • Difficulty 2

1	tablespoon almond oil	2	cups (500 ml) heavy (double) cream
1/2	cup (125 ml) very strong black coffee	6	large egg yolks
1 1/4	cups (250 g) sugar		Coffee beans, to decorate
1	vanilla pod		

1. Oil a 6-cup (1.5-liter) pudding mold with the oil.

2. Combine the coffee, sugar, and vanilla in a small saucepan over medium heat and bring to a boil. Simmer for 2–3 minutes then remove from the heat. Let cool. Discard the vanilla pod when cool.

3. Beat the egg yolks in the top pan of a double boiler with an electric mixer on high speed while gradually adding the cooled sugar syrup. Place over barely simmering water and beat for 5 minutes. Remove from the heat and beat until thick, creamy, and cool.

4. Beat 1 1/2 cups (375 ml) of cream in a large bowl with an electric mixer on high speed until thick. Fold the cream into the egg mixture. Spoon into the prepared mold and freeze for at least 4 hours.

5. Beat the remaining cream just before serving and decorate the semifreddo. Top with the coffee beans.

TEA semifreddo

Serves 4–6 • Preparation 20 minutes + 6 hours to freeze
Cooking 15 minutes • Difficulty 2

1	tablespoon almond oil	6	sugar cubes
1/2	cup (125 ml) water	1	cup (200 g) sugar
2	teaspoons loose tea leaves	6	large egg yolks
1	vanilla pod	2	cups (500 ml) heavy (double) cream
2	organic oranges	3	tablespoons white rum

1. Brush a 6-cup (1.5-liter) pudding mold with the oil.

2. Bring the water to a boil. Remove from the heat. Add the tea and vanilla. Set aside for 10 minutes.

3. Rub the oranges all over with the sugar cubes so that they absorb the orange color and flavor.

4. Strain the tea and return to the saucepan with the sugar cubes and sugar. Place over low heat and simmer until the mixture reaches 230-233°F (110-111°C) on an instant read thermometer. Let cool.

5. Beat the egg yolks in a medium bowl, gradually adding the tea and sugar mixture until thick.

6. Beat the cream until thick. Fold into the egg and sugar mixture. Fold in the rum. Spoon into the mold and freeze for at least 6 hours.

ZABAGLIONE semifreddo

Serves 6 • Preparation 20 minutes + 6 hours to freeze
Cooking 10–15 minutes • Difficulty 2

8	large egg yolks	2	cups (500 ml) heavy (double) cream
1	cup (200 g) sugar		Langue de chat cookies or wafers, to serve
1	cup (250 ml) Marsala wine		

1. Beat the egg yolks and sugar in a large bowl with an electric mixer on high speed until very pale and creamy. Gradually beat in the Marsala, 1 tablespoon at a time.

2. Place the mixture in a double boiler over barely simmering water and beat until thick and creamy, 10–15 minutes. Remove from the heat and let cool.

3. Beat the cream in a large bowl with an electric mixer on high speed until thick.

4. Set aside 1/4 cup (60 ml) of the zabaglione. Fold the cream into the remaining zabaglione.

5. Oil six small ramekins with almond oil. Spoon the semifreddo into the ramekins. Freeze for at least 6 hours.

6. Just before serving, turn the semifreddo desserts out onto serving dishes and spoon the reserved zabaglione over the top.

This traditional Sicilian ice cream cake consists of a sponge cake lining moistened with fruit juice or liqueur and filled with frozen ricotta cheese, candied fruit, and chocolate. It is topped with marzipan and decorated with more candied fruit. In our recipe we have flavored the marzipan with orange flower water, but you can also color it with green food coloring to resemble the traditional pistachio topping. It is not a simple dessert, but really worth the effort!

SICILIAN cassata

1¼ cups (250 g) sugar
½ cup (125 ml) water
1 vanilla pod
1 pound (500 g) fresh ricotta cheese, strained
5 ounces (150 g) dark chocolate, chopped
3 cups (300 g) mixed candied fruit + extra, to decorate (optional)
2 tablespoons pistachio nuts, shelled
2 tablespoons Maraschino or kirsch liqueur
1 storebought 12-inch (30-cm) sponge cake, thinly sliced
½ cup (125 g) apricot preserves (jam), warmed
8 ounces (250 g) marzipan
2 tablespoons orange flower water

Serves 6–8 • Preparation 30 minutes + 30 minutes to macerate + 4 hours to freeze • Cooking 2–3 minutes • Difficulty 3

1. Combine the sugar, water, and vanilla pod in a heavy-based pan and simmer over low heat until the sugar is dissolved, 2–3 minutes. Set aside to cool.

2. Beat the ricotta vigorously with a spatula, then add the cooled syrup gradually, stirring until the mixture becomes soft and creamy. Gradually stir the chocolate and candied fruit into the ricotta, then add the nuts and liqueur.

3. Line the bottom and sides of a 10-inch (25-cm) springform pan with slices of sponge, using a little of the apricot preserves to stick them to the pan. Fill with the ricotta mixture, spreading it evenly. Cover with slices of sponge. Freeze for at least 4 hours.

4. Knead the marzipan until softened, then gradually knead in the orange flower water. Place the cake on a serving plate. Spread with the remaining apricot preserves. Decorate with extra candied fruit, if liked.

If you liked this recipe, you will love these as well.

COCONUT ice cream bombe

CHOCOLATE CANDIED FRUIT parfait

SICILIAN ice cream cake

COCONUT ice cream bombe

½ cup (50 g) candied orange peel, chopped
¼ cup (60 ml) rum
⅓ cup (40 g) shredded (desiccated) coconut
¼ cup (30 g) blanched almonds
4 ounces (120 g) dark chocolate, grated
1 recipe Egg Cream Ice Cream (see page 12), softened
¾ cup (200 ml) heavy (double) cream

Serves 6–8 • Preparation 30 minutes + 30 minutes to soak + 9 hours to freeze • Cooking 5 minutes • Difficulty 3

1. Line a 6-cup (1.5-liter) pudding mold with plastic wrap (cling film) and place in the freezer.

2. Soak the orange peel in a small bowl with the rum for 30 minutes, then drain. Chop the almonds coarsely.

3. Put the ice cream in a large bowl and stir in the orange peel. Spoon two-thirds into the mold, spreading it over the bottom and sides. Freeze for 1 hour.

4. Whip the cream until thick. Stir in half the coconut, the chopped almonds, and half the chocolate. Spoon into the center of the mold. Freeze for 1 hour.

5. Spread the remaining ice cream over the cream mixture. Freeze for 4 hours.

6. Melt the remaining chocolate in a double boiler over barely simmering water. Turn the bombe out onto a serving dish. Top with the melted chocolate and remaining coconut.

MARBLED ice cream bombe

- 4 ounces (125 g) dark chocolate, coarsely chopped
- 9 tablespoons (135 g) butter
- 4 ounces (125 g) milk chocolate, coarsely chopped
- 4 ounces (125 g) white chocolate, coarsely chopped
- 3/4 cup (100 g) raisins
- 1/4 cup (60 ml) dark rum
- 1 recipe Egg Cream Ice Cream (see page 12), softened
- 1 cup (120 g) pistachios, chopped

Serves 6-8 • Preparation 30 minutes + 9 hours to freeze • Cooking 15 minutes • Difficulty 3

1. Line an 8-cup (2-liter) pudding mold with plastic wrap (cling film) and place in the freezer.

2. Melt the dark chocolate with 3 tablespoons of butter in a double boiler over barely simmering water. Repeat with the milk and white chocolates, melting each type of chocolate with 3 tablespoons of butter.

3. Spread spoonfuls of the three chocolates in the bowl, smearing them up the sides to create an even coating and swirling them together to create a marbled effect. Freeze until the chocolate is set, about 1 hour.

4. Simmer the raisins in the rum in a saucepan over medium heat for 3-4 minutes. Set aside to cool.

5. Mix the ice cream, raisins, and pistachios in a large bowl. Carefully spoon into the chocolate shell, cover with plastic wrap, and freeze 8 hours.

If you are short of time, use store-bought chocolate and vanilla ice cream to prepare this cake. You will need about 3 cups (750 g) of each flavor. Vary the flavors of the ice cream according to what you like or what you have in the freezer.

CHOCOLATE & AROMATIC ice cream cake

Cake
1   tablespoon almond oil
12   ounces (350 g) amaretti cookies
1   recipe Chocolate Ice Cream (without the mint, see page 36), softened
1   recipe Aromatic Ice Cream (see pages 10), softened

Ganache
1   cup (250 ml) heavy (double) cream
1   tablespoon corn (golden) syrup
8   ounces dark chocolate, chopped

Serves: 6–8 • Preparation 30 minutes + 5 hours to freeze • Cooking 5 minutes • Difficulty 2

Cake
1. Brush a 9-inch (23-cm) springform pan with the oil. Crush the amaretti cookies to make coarse crumbs. Press half the crumbs over the bottom and $1/2$ inch (1 cm) up sides of the pan. Spread the chocolate ice cream evenly over the crust. Sprinkle with the remaining crumbs. Freeze for 1 hour.

2. Spread the aromatic ice cream evenly over the cake and freeze for at least 4 hours or until firm.

Ganache
1. Bring the cream and corn syrup to a boil in a small saucepan. Remove from the heat and stir in the chocolate. Let sit for 5 minutes, then stir until thick. Let cool.

2. Spread the chocolate ganache over the cake. Let harden for 5 minutes before serving.

If you liked this recipe, you will love these as well.

CHOCOLATE COOKIE
ice cream cake

ICE CREAM MERINGUE
torte

BLACK FOREST
ice cream cake

CHOCOLATE SEMIFREDDO
with cherry compote

Semifreddo

2	cups (500 ml) milk
6	large egg yolks
$^3/_4$	cup (150 g) sugar
1	teaspoon vanilla extract (essence)
$^1/_3$	cup (50 g) unsweetened cocoa powder
$^1/_4$	cup (60 ml) water
2	cups (500 ml) heavy (double) cream + extra whipped cream to serve

Cherry Compote

1	pound (500 g) fresh cherries, pitted
1	cup (200 g) sugar
$^1/_4$	cup (60 ml) kirsch
$^1/_2$	teaspoon cornstarch (cornflour)
1	tablespoon water

Serves 4-6 • Preparation 20 minutes + 12 hours to freeze • Cooking 15–20 minutes • Difficulty 2

Semifreddo

1. Bring the milk to a boil in a heavy-based saucepan over medium heat. Remove from the heat.

2. Beat the egg yolks, sugar, and vanilla in a large bowl with an electric mixer on high speed until pale and creamy. Gradually pour in the hot milk, beating constantly with a wooden spoon. Return to the saucepan. Simmer over very low heat, stirring constantly, until it just coats the back of the spoon. Do not let the mixture boil. Pour into a bowl.

3. Mix the cocoa with the water in a cup. Stir into the egg mixture. Let cool completely, stirring often. Beat the cream until thick. Fold into the egg mixture. Spoon into a 6-cup (1.5-liter) pudding mold. Freeze overnight.

Cherry Compote

1. Stir the cherries, sugar, and kirsch in a pan over medium-low heat until the cherries are tender, 8–10 minutes.

2. Mix the cornstarch and water in a cup. Stir into the cherries. Simmer until thickened, 2–3 minutes. Serve with the semifreddo and extra cream.

CHOCOLATE CANDIED FRUIT parfait

⅓ cup (60 g) candied peel, chopped

⅓ cup (60 g) candied cherries, chopped

¼ cup (60 ml) Grand Marnier

1 recipe Chocolate Ice Cream (without the mint, see page 36), softened

¾ cup (150 g) sugar

¼ cup (60 ml) water

3 large egg whites

1 cup (250 ml) heavy (double) cream

Serves 6 • Preparation 20 minutes + 6 hours to freeze • Cooking 5 minutes • Difficulty 2

1. Combine the candied peel, cherries, and Grand Marnier in a bowl. Line an 9 x 5-inch (24 x 10-cm) loaf pan with plastic wrap (cling film). Spread the bottom and sides of the pan with three-quarters of the ice cream. Freeze for 1 hour.

2. Combine ½ cup (100 g) of sugar in a saucepan with the water over medium heat and bring to a boil. Stir until the sugar has dissolved, 2–3 minutes. Let cool completely.

3. Beat the egg whites in a large bowl with an electric mixer until soft peaks form. Add the remaining sugar and beat until stiff. Beat in the sugar syrup until thick and glossy.

4. Whip the cream until thick. Fold the cream and candied fruit mixture into the egg-white mixture. Spoon into the prepared chocolate ice cream case. Freeze for 1 hour. Cover with the remaining chocolate ice cream. Freeze for 4 hours.

This is a great cake for a children's birthday party.

CHOCOLATE COOKIE ice cream cake

1	(18-ounce/600 g) package small chocolate chip cookies (about 40 cookies)
1/4	cup (60 g) butter, melted
1	cup (250 g) wild cherry preserves (jam)
5	ounces (150 g) dark chocolate
1	recipe Vanilla Ice Cream (see page 8), softened
3/4	cup (200 ml) heavy (double) cream
	Fresh or candied (glacé) cherries to decorate

Serves 6–8 • Preparation 30 minutes + 4 hours to freeze • Cooking 10–15 minutes • Difficulty 2

1. Crush just over half the cookies (about 22–24) and combine in a bowl with the butter. Press the mixture into the base of a 9-inch (23-cm) springform pan. Spread with the cherry preserves. Stand the remaining cookies around the edges of the pan, pressing them into the cookie base.

2. Melt the chocolate in a double boiler over barely simmering water. Stir four-fifths of the chocolate into the ice cream and stir a little. Do not overstir; you want small lumps of chocolate in the vanilla (not a pale brown ice cream). Spread the ice cream in the pan over the cherry preserves.

3. Whip the cream until thickened and spread over the cake in the pan. Drizzle with the remaining melted chocolate and decorate with the cherries.

4. Freeze until firm, about 4 hours.

If you liked this recipe, you will love these as well.

CHOCOLATE & AROMATIC ice cream cake

GINGERSNAP & CREAM cookie sandwiches

STRAWBERRY ice cream cake

GINGERSNAP & CREAM cookie sandwiches

1   cup (150 g) all-purpose (plain) flour
1   teaspoon baking soda (bicarbonate of soda)
$1/2$ teaspoon ground cinnamon
1   teaspoon ground ginger
$1/8$ teaspoon freshly ground white pepper
$1/4$ teaspoon ground allspice
$1/4$ teaspoon salt
4   ounces (125 g) unsalted butter, softened
$1/2$ cup (100 g) sugar
$1/4$ cup (50 g) firmly packed light brown sugar
1   large egg
3   tablespoons molasses
1   recipe Egg Cream Ice Cream (see page 12)

Serves 12 • Preparation 20 minutes + 5 hours to chill • Cooking 10–12 minutes • Difficulty 2

1. Sift the flour, baking soda, cinnamon, ginger, white pepper, allspice, and salt into a medium bowl.

2. Beat the butter, $1/4$ cup (50 g) of sugar, and the brown sugar until creamy. Stir in the egg, followed by the molasses. Stir in the mixed dry ingredients. Refrigerate until very firm, at least 3 hours.

3. Divide the dough in half, wrap each half in plastic wrap (cling film), and refrigerate for at least 2 hours (up to 4 days). Roll the dough into two 9-inch (23-cm)-long logs.

4. Preheat the oven to 350°F (180°C/gas 4). Line 3 baking sheets with parchment paper. Cut the dough into $1/2$-inch (1-cm) slices. Put the remaining $1/4$ cup (50 g) sugar in a bowl. Coat the cookies with the sugar. Place on the prepared sheets. Bake for 10–12 minutes. Let cool on a rack

5. Place 12 cookies on a work surface. Place a scoop of ice cream on each. Top with a second cookie.

ICE CREAM meringue torte

$^1/_3$ cup (50 g) confectioners' (icing) sugar

$^1/_4$ cup (50 g) superfine (caster) sugar

2 large egg whites

1 recipe Egg Cream Ice Cream (see page 12), softened

1 recipe Double Chocolate Chip Ice Cream (see page 36), softened

2 cups (500 ml) heavy (double) cream

Dark chocolate, grated to decorate

Serves 6 • Preparation 45 minutes + 2 hours to freeze • Cooking 90 minutes • Difficulty 3

1. Preheat the oven to 200°F (110°C/gas $^1/_2$). Mix both sugars in a bowl. Beat the egg whites in a large bowl with an electric mixer on high speed. Beat in the sugar mixture gradually, until the mixture is thick and glossy.

2. Line two baking sheets with parchment paper. Trace three 9-inch (23-cm) circles onto the parchment. Spoon the meringue onto the baking sheets to make three disks about $^1/_2$-inch (1 cm) thick. Bake until dry and crisp, about 90 minutes. Remove from the oven and let cool.

3. Line a 10-inch (25-cm) springform pan with parchment. Place one meringue disk in the pan. Spread with a $^1/_2$-inch (1-cm) layer of egg cream ice cream. Add another meringue disk. Spread with a $^1/_2$-inch (1-cm) layer of chocolate ice cream. Top with the remaining meringue. Freeze for 2 hours.

4. Whip the cream until thick. Unmold the torte and spread the top and sides with cream. Top with the chocolate.

This is the frozen version of the classic German layer cake. If you are short of time, use store-bought chocolate ice cream. You will need about 4 cups (1 kg).

BLACK FOREST ice cream cake

Cake Base

3/4 cup (125 g) all-purpose (plain) flour

1/3 cup (50 g) unsweetened cocoa powder

1 teaspoon baking powder

1/3 cup (90 g) butter, softened

3/4 cup (150 g) superfine (caster) sugar

1/2 teaspoon vanilla extract (essence)

1 large egg

1/2 cup (125 ml) sour cream

Filling

2 tablespoons kirsch (cherry brandy)

1 recipe Chocolate Ice Cream (see page 36), softened

2 cups (400 g) canned pitted black cherries, drained

Topping

1 1/2 cups (375 ml) heavy (double) cream

2 tablespoon confectioners' (icing) sugar

3 ounces (90 g) dark chocolate, shaved, to decorate

Serves 8 • Preparation 30 minutes + 9 hours to cool and freeze
Cooking 25–30 minutes • Difficulty 3

Cake Base

1. Preheat the oven to 350°F (180°C/gas 4). Lightly grease a 9-inch (23 cm) springform pan. Line the base with parchment paper. Sift the flour, cocoa, and baking powder into a small bowl.

2. Beat the butter, sugar, and vanilla in a medium bowl until pale and creamy. Beat in the egg until just blended. With mixer on low, beat in the flour mixture and sour cream.

3. Spoon the batter into the prepared pan. Bake for 25–30 minutes, until a skewer comes out clean when inserted into the center. Let cool in the pan for 10 minutes, then turn out onto a wire rack and let cool completely.

Filling

1. Stir the kirsch into the ice cream. Line the sides of a clean 9-inch (23-cm) springform pan with parchment paper. Place the cooled sponge base back in the pan. Sprinkle with the cherries. Spoon the ice-cream over the cherries and smooth the top. Cover with plastic wrap (cling film) and freeze for 4 hours.

Topping

1. Beat the cream and confectioners' sugar in a medium bowl until thick. Remove the cake from the pan and spread the cream over the top and sides. Decorate with the chocolate shavings and freeze until solid, at least 4 more hours.

NEAPOLITAN ice cream cake

Serves 6–8 • Preparation 30 minutes + 1 hour to soak + 5 hours to freeze • Difficulty 2

1	cup (100 g) candied (glacé) cherries, coarsely chopped + 6-8 extra to decorate	1	recipe Cardamom Ice Cream (see page 16), softened
1/2	cup (120 ml) kirsch (cherry brandy)	1	recipe Double Chocolate Chip Ice Cream (see page 36), softened
1	(9-inch/23-cm) store-bought sponge cake		

1. Soak the cherries in the kirsch for 1 hour.

2. Line a 9-inch (23-cm) springform pan with parchment paper. Put the sponge cake in the prepared pan. Freeze for 1 hour.

3. Drain the cherries, reserving the kirsch. Drizzle the kirsch over the cake. Spread with the cardamom ice cream. Arrange the cherries on top and spread with the chocolate ice cream. Freeze for 4 hours.

4. Dip the pan briefly into cold water. Invert onto a serving plate. Decorate each slice with the extra candied cherries.

RICOTTA parfait

Serves 6 • Preparation 15 minutes + 3 hours to freeze Difficulty 1

1	pound (500 g) fresh ricotta cheese, strained	1/2	cup (60 g) raisins
1/2	cup (60 g) walnuts, chopped	1/2	cup (100 g) sugar
1/2	cup (60 g) pistachios, chopped	2	tablespoons kirsch (or other fruit liqueur)
1/2	cup (60 g) dark chocolate, chopped	1	tablespoon finely grated lemon zest
1/2	cup (50 g) mixed candied fruit, chopped	1	tablespoon finely grated orange zest
		1	teaspoon vanilla extract (essence)

1. Line an 8½ x 4½-inch (22 x 10-cm) loaf pan with aluminum foil, letting the edges overhang.

2. Combine the ricotta, walnuts, pistachios, chocolate, candied fruit, raisins, sugar, liqueur, lemon and orange zest, and vanilla in a large bowl and mix well. Spoon the mixture into the prepared pan. Freeze for at least 3 hours.

3. Turn out onto a serving dish and carefully remove the foil.

STRAWBERRY ice cream cake

Serves 6–8 • Preparation 20 minutes + 7 hours to freeze Difficulty 2

1	store-bought 10-inch (25-cm) sponge cake	8	small, plain meringues, crumbled
1/4	cup (60 ml) Chambord (raspberry liqueur)		Pistachios, coarsely chopped, to serve
1	recipe Aromatic Ice Cream (see page 10), softened		Fresh strawberries, sliced, to serve
1	recipe Strawberry Spumone (see page 69)		Whipped cream, to serve

1. Butter a 10-inch (25-cm) springform pan. Put the sponge cake in the bottom of the prepared pan. Drizzle with the Chambord. Freeze for 1 hour.

2. Spread with an even layer of aromatic ice cream. Sprinkle with the pieces of crumbled meringue. Cover with an even layer of the strawberry spumone. Freeze for at least 6 hours.

3. Unmold the cake and transfer to a serving dish. Decorate with the pistachios, strawberries, and cream and serve at once.

SICILIAN ice cream cake

Serves 6–8 • Preparation 30 minutes + 30 minutes to macerate + 4 hours to freeze • Difficulty 2

1	recipe Vanilla Ice Cream (see page 8), softened	1	large egg white
1	teaspoon green food coloring	5	tablespoons confectioners' (icing) sugar
1	cup (100 g) mixed candied fruit, chopped	1	cup (250 ml) heavy (double) cream
1/4	cup (60 ml) white rum		

1. Put a 6-cup (1.5-liter) pudding mold in the freezer for 1 hour. Stir the green food coloring into the softened ice cream. Place the chopped candied fruit in a small bowl and pour the rum over the top. Let macerate for 30 minutes.

2. Line the mold with the green ice cream. Use a spoon dipped in ice water to smooth into an even layer.

3. Beat the egg white and confectioners' sugar with an electric mixer on high speed until stiff. Beat the cream in a separate bowl until thick then fold into the egg white mixture. Stir in the candied fruit and rum.

4. Fill the center of the cake with the cream mixture and freeze for at least 4 hours. To serve, dip the mold quickly into hot water. Put a serving plate over the mold and turn the cake onto it.

LEMON & PASSION FRUIT parfait

8	large egg yolks
1	cup (250 ml) passion fruit pulp (about 20 passion fruit)
1	cup (200 g) sugar
1/4	cup (60 ml) freshly squeezed lemon juice
1 1/4	cups (300 ml) heavy (double) cream
1/2	cup (125 ml) half-and-half (single) cream

Serves 4-6 • Preparation 20 minutes + 12 hours to freeze • Cooking 15 minutes • Difficulty 1

1. Line a 3 x 9-inch (8 x 23-cm) loaf pan with plastic wrap (cling film), leaving a 2-inch (5-cm) overhang. Strain 3/4 cup (180 ml) of passion fruit pulp through a fine-mesh sieve.

2. Combine with the sugar and lemon juice in a medium saucepan over medium heat and simmer until the sugar has dissolved, 3-4 minutes. Let cool. Beat the egg yolks until pale and creamy. Gradually pour the syrup into the egg yolks, beating until thick and cool, 4-5 minutes.

3. Combine both types of cream in a medium bowl and beat until soft peaks form. Fold into the egg yolk mixture.

4. Pour into the pan, cover with plastic wrap, and freeze overnight. Drizzle with the remaining passion fruit pulp just before serving.

WHITE CHOCOLATE & STRAWBERRY *parfait*

8   large egg yolks

1¼   cups (300 ml) heavy (double)
     cream

4   ounces (125 g) white
     chocolate, coarsely chopped

1   cup (200 g) sugar

2½   cups (375 g) strawberries
     + 6-8 extra, halved, to
     decorate

2   tablespoons freshly squeezed
     lemon juice

½   cup (125 ml) half-and-half
     (single) cream

Serves 4-6 • Preparation 30 minutes + 12 hours to freeze • Cooking 15
minutes • Difficulty 1

1. Line a 3 x 9-inch (8 x 23-cm) loaf pan with plastic wrap
   (cling film), leaving a 2-inch (5-cm) overhang. Beat the egg
   yolks in a medium bowl until pale and creamy.

2. Put ¼ cup (60 ml) of the heavy cream in a small saucepan
   and bring to a boil. Put the chocolate in a small heatproof
   bowl and pour the hot cream over the top, stirring until
   smooth. Set aside.

3. Combine the sugar, strawberries, and lemon juice in a small
   saucepan over medium-low heat and simmer until the
   strawberries are soft and the liquid is syrupy, 3-4 minutes.
   Transfer to a food processor and blend until smooth. Press
   through a fine-mesh sieve. Gradually pour the strawberry
   syrup into the egg yolks, beating until thick and cool, 4-5
   minutes. Stir in the melted chocolate mixture.

4. Combine the remaining heavy cream and half-and-half in a
   medium bowl and beat until soft peaks form. Fold into the
   strawberry mixture. Pour into the pan, cover with plastic
   wrap, and freeze overnight.

5. To serve, slice using a hot knife. Decorate with strawberries.

BIRTHDAY ice cream cake

116

Ice Cream

3 cups (750 ml) milk
1 vanilla pod
  Zest of 1 lemon, in 1 long piece
6 large egg yolks
1 cup (200 g) sugar
3 tablespoons Cointreau
1/2 cup (90 g) heavy (double) cream
3 ounces (90 g) dark chocolate, grated

Meringue

2 large egg whites
1 cup (150 g) confectioners' (icing) sugar

To Assemble

1 store-bought 9-inch (23-cm) sponge cake
5 ounces (150 g) dark chocolate
2 tablespoons Cointreau
3/4 cup (200 ml) heavy (double) cream

Serves 6–8 • Preparation 30 minutes + time to churn • Cooking 1 hour 45 minutes • Difficulty 3

Ice Cream

1. Heat the milk with the vanilla pod and lemon zest in a heavy-based saucepan over medium heat and bring to a boil. Remove from the heat and discard the vanilla pod.

2. Beat the egg yolks and sugar until pale and creamy. Pour the hot milk mixture into the egg yolk mixture, beating constantly with a wooden spoon. Return to the pan. Simmer over low heat, beating constantly, until the mixture coats the back of the spoon. Do not let it boil.

3. Pour equal parts of the mixture into two separate bowls and let cool completely. Stir 2 tablespoons of Cointreau into one bowl. Transfer to your ice cream machine and churn according to the manufacturers' instructions.

4. Beat the cream until thick. Fold into the second bowl with the chocolate. Transfer to your ice cream machine and churn according to the manufacturers' instructions.

Meringue

1. Preheat the oven to 225°F (110°C/gas 1/2). Line a baking sheet with parchment paper. Put a 9-inch (23-cm) springform pan on the paper and draw a line around it.

2. Beat the egg whites and confectioners' sugar in a medium bowl with an electric mixer on high speed until stiff. Spread the meringue in the disk on the paper. Bake until crisp and dry, about 90 minutes. Let cool completely.

To Assemble

1. Line the 9-inch (23-cm) springform pan with parchment paper. Spread the chocolate chip ice cream on the bottom. Top with the meringue (trim the edges if it has spread during cooking). Cover with the sponge cake. Drizzle with the Cointreau. Top with the Cointreau ice cream. Cover with plastic wrap and freeze for 4 hours.

2. Melt the chocolate in a double boiler over barely simmering water. Let cool. Place most of the cooled chocolate into a piping bag with a plain nozzle and pipe out 8–12 small disks. Place in the refrigerator to set.

3. Beat the cream until thick. Fold in the remaining chocolate. Unmold the cake and decorate with the chocolate cream and disks of chocolate.

COFFEE ice cream ring

Ice Cream

2	cups (500 ml) milk
1/2	cup (125 ml) heavy (double) cream
4	large egg yolks
1/3	cup (75 g) sugar
2	teaspoons vanilla extract (essence)
1/4	cup (30 g) confectioners' (icing) sugar
4	ounces (125 g) dark chocolate, coarsely chopped
1/2	cup (125 ml) strong black coffee, cold

Decoration

1	cup (250 ml) heavy (double) cream
2	tablespoons brandy
2	tablespoons confectioners' (icing) sugar
1	tablespoon whole coffee beans

Serves 6 • Preparation 30 minutes + 30 minutes to chill + time to churn
Cooking 5–10 minutes • Difficulty 2

Ice Cream

1. Combine the milk and cream in a heavy-based saucepan over medium heat and bring to a boil.

2. Beat the egg yolks and sugar with an electric mixer on high speed until pale and creamy. Pour the hot milk mixture into the egg mixture, stirring constantly with a spoon. Return to the saucepan. Simmer over low heat, stirring constantly, until the mixture coats the back of the spoon. Do not let it boil.

3. Remove from the heat. Stir in the vanilla. Chill in the refrigerator for 30 minutes. Transfer to an ice cream machine and churn according to the manufacturer's instructions.

4. Divide the ice cream equally between two bowls. Stir the chocolate into one bowl and the coffee into the other. Place alternate spoonfuls into an oiled 9-inch (23-cm) ring mold. Freeze for 1 hour.

Decoration

1. Beat the cream, brandy, and confectioners' sugar until thick. Unmold the cake onto a serving plate. Top with the cream and coffee beans.

RICOTTA & STRAWBERRY dome

2   large limes, peeled and very thinly sliced

$^3/_4$ cup (150 g) sugar

$^1/_2$ cup (125 ml) lemon liqueur

4   large egg yolks

1   teaspoon vanilla extract (essence)

1   pound (500 g) fresh ricotta cheese, strained

2   tablespoons finely grated organic orange zest

14   ounces (400 g) chopped fresh strawberries

1   cup (250 ml) heavy (double) cream

Serves 6 • Preparation 20 minutes + 2 hours to soak + 4 hours to freeze
Cooking 5 minutes • Difficulty 3

1. Put the limes in a large bowl. Add $^1/_4$ cup (50 g) of sugar and the lemon liqueur. Soak for 2 hours.

2. Beat the egg yolks, remaining $^1/_2$ cup (100 g) sugar, and vanilla until pale and creamy. Transfer to a double boiler over barely simmering water and stir constantly until the mixture coats the back of the spoon. Let cool completely.

3. Mix the ricotta, orange zest, strawberries, and egg yolk mixture in a large bowl.

4. Beat the cream until thick. Fold into the ricotta mixture.

5. Rinse a domed 6-cup (1.5-liter) pudding mold with cold water. Line with the limes, overlapping slightly. Carefully spoon in the ricotta mixture, taking care not to dislodge the limes. Freeze for 4 hours.

INDEX

First published in the UK in 2012 by
Apple Press
7 Greenland Street
London NW1 0ND
United Kingdom
www.apple-press.com

This book was conceived, edited and designed by
McRae Publishing Ltd, London

NOTE TO OUR READERS
Eating eggs or egg whites that are not completely cooked poses the possibility
of salmonella food poisoning. The risk is greater for pregnant women, the elderly,
the very young, and persons with impaired immune systems. If you are concerned
about salmonella, you can use reconstituted powdered egg whites or pasteurized eggs.

Project Director Anne McRae
Art Director Marco Nardi

ICE CREAMS & SORBETS
Photography Brent Parker Jones
Text Carla Bardi
Editing Foreign Concept
Food Styling Lee Blaylock
Food Styling Assistant Rochelle Seator
Prop Styling Lee Blaylock
Layouts Filippo Delle Monache

ISBN 978-1-84543-443-4

Printed in China